EMPOWER
YOUR
SUBCONSCIOUS

EMPOWER
YOUR
SUBCONSCIOUS

HOW TO UNLOCK 96% OF YOUR BRAIN

KURT GASSNER

My-mindguide.com

Empower Your Subconscious
Kurt Gassner

Impressum
My-mindguide – The publishing trademarke of trendguide Capital GmbH, Klenzestr. 42a, 80469 Munich, Germany.

Reg. Nr. HRB Munich 206639, VAT 152 123 159, CEO: Kurt Friedrich Gassner
Web: www.my-mindguide.com, mail: gassner@my-mindguide.com

Paperback ISBN: 978-3-949978-57-9
Ebook ISBN: 978-3-949978-58-6
Hardback ISBN: 978-3-949978-59-3

Table of Contents

The Ice Mountain

Mind Model

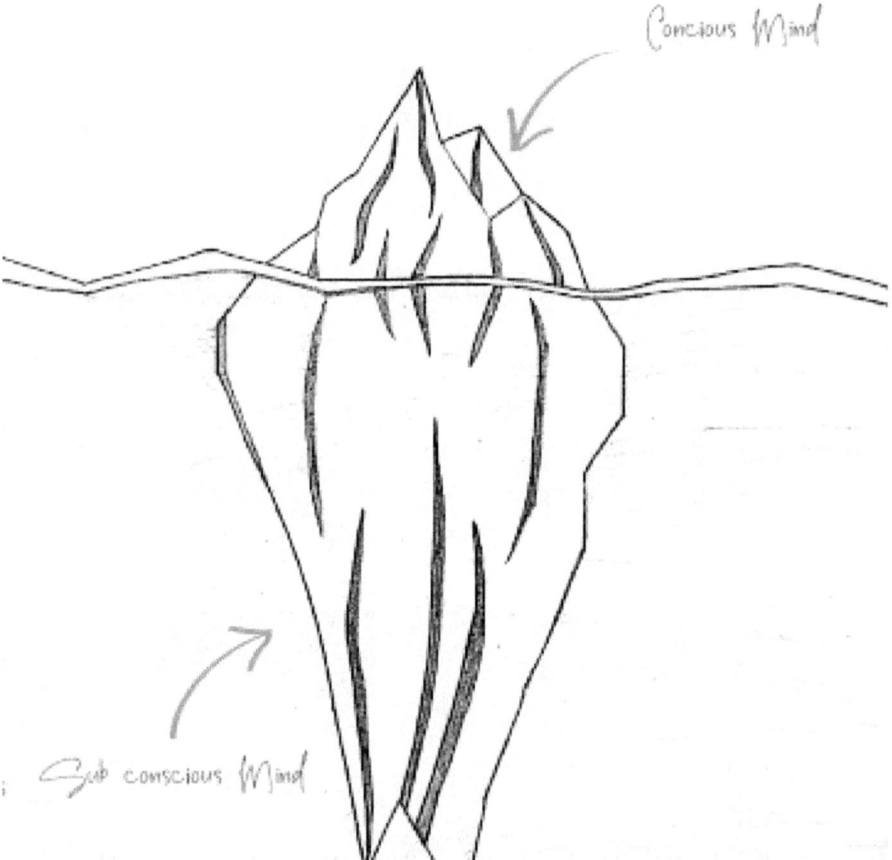

My-mindguide.com

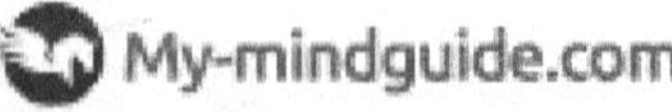

Empower your subconscious

The subconscious mind acts as the second brain. It is the primary driver of everything throughout your life.

Improving the capacity to strengthen the link between your subconscious and conscious minds is an effective tool that can increase your wealth, happiness, and prosperity. Truly, the subconscious mind is the best method of controlling everything in your life, therefore enhancing the brain's ability to communicate between the subconscious and conscious minds will help you attain wellness and a better quality of life.

The subconscious mind functions as an information storage facility, housing all of the details that are not present in your conscious mind, including your memories, thoughts from the past, and learned abilities. Everything you have been through, contemplated, or performed is stored in this location. It can also act as your guide to life, constantly monitoring the information received through the senses to detect potential dangers or opportunities. This information is then relayed to the brain.

The link between the subconscious brain and the conscious brain is bi-directional. Whenever you experience an emotion, idea, thought, or image that you have seen or felt in the past, it could be the subconscious brain communicating with your consciousness. This is achievable via the notion of auto-suggestion. This book will help you learn how your unconscious can be a powerful tool. It will show you how to best harness your subconscious using various methods to achieve your goals.

Join me to learn to converse with your unconscious mind, and in the process, lead it in the direction of the life path you most desire. You are in control.

How Our Mind Works

We are entangled in an inexplicably complex mystery when we speak of the mind. In principle, we all recognize its presence, but it is inaccessible and often not heard or understood in the way it could be. Most people think the mind is only made up of the physical portion composed of the brain. The brain helps us understand various phenomena, such as vision transmitted by the eyes and information sent via the other senses. It is the center of knowledge. However, the entire mind is a separate aspect that constantly swarms around us, circling us like the spirit or soul. It goes by different names, but the mind controls our lives and guides us in our decision-making processes regardless of the terminology.

What meal should we eat at the restaurant? What dress should I purchase? The mind constantly makes such decisions, and we associate our minds with who we are as individuals. Also, since we are the keepers of our own minds, the brain is ours. Many prefer to use the term "consciousness," which is more evocative and can evoke different meanings when understood in detail. While we sleep, our mind is not really in a state of rest. Instead, the subconscious mind is active as we experience dreams, and we can often recall these dreams in the morning. Specific themes and concepts are transmitted through dreams, and awakening can lead us to believe that we have mastered new realms of knowledge and uncovered new and potentially valuable insights.

With all the wisdom of the human race, we have accepted that the mind can be a formidable container that functions similarly to a hard disk. Information can be saved, deleted, processed, stored, or even reactivated. The way we interact with the mind is up to each of us, using it either for good or evil because we are all a part of the cosmic pattern.

a. The Conscious Mind

Every day, maneuvering our waking hours depends on the conscious mind, which is consciousness itself, representing logic, reasoning, and common sense. Our conscious minds would be amazed at the actual ability of the entire mind, which appears to reflect the expanse of the universe. There is nothing too big and no concept too complex or extraordinary that the mind cannot handle it. When we look at the accomplishments of individuals throughout time, focusing on the works that came from the minds of writers, inventors, historians, philosophers, and scientists, it is incredible. These accomplishments were all made possible by the power of the mind.

As we work and play every day, going out, eating, and talking, and as we enjoy our vacations, deliver speeches, sit at the computer, or drive our vehicles, our conscious minds are working. Doing these things could be risky if the alert conscious mind suffers even for a few seconds, such as driving or operating complex machinery. When we say conscious, it means things in our awareness. Every little decision in life is a result of our conscious mind working. The conscious mind is formed at an early age and develops until death. A child's awareness is immature and improves with time and education. The conscious mind is understood much more effectively when compared to the unconscious mind, which is the subconscious mind. The subconscious mind is made up of the memories of the past, hidden thoughts and emotions, dreams, and desires. These are all tucked away within the unconscious mind. The conscious mind is an all-seeing eye, functioning at every moment of our lives, acting as the mirror showing truth and awareness. The subconscious mind is something else entirely.

b. The Subconscious Mind: An Introduction

The involuntary mind, which plays a vital role in regulating critical life processes such as breathing and heartbeat, could be called "the unconscious" mind. While the conscious mind dwells on the surface, the subconscious mind is found amidst deeper waters—and is much more obscure than the water's surface. The subconscious is dark, suffocated, and stifled, while the conscious mind is translucent and crystal clear. We are often afraid of the subconscious mind due to the fear of the unknown or poorly understood. We know that it could prompt us to act in ways the conscious mind would not, even committing a crime or other wrongdoing. Keep in mind, many criminal cases are believed to be a result of the unconscious self in action. Memories, emotions, and beliefs are stored in the brain's unconscious. The subconscious operates blindly, without reason or logic, which can sometimes be problematic. If the unconscious takes over our thinking, we could get into trouble.

There are psychological issues that the subconscious mind can trigger. For instance, split personality disorder is thought to result from a problem within the brain. In this case, two distinct sets of traits control the mind, and each manifests in different circumstances. Because our subconscious mind can control emotions, it implies that this is what determines our personality. Sudden urges of worry, fear, hate, and anger can lead to challenging situations. Thus, it is best to practice caution while experiencing stressful situations. Certain philosophies focus on learning and honing practices to control the mind, understanding that the mind is the very foundation of everything. Meditation exercises play a substantial part in relaxing the mind and revealing new ideas and a deeper understanding. Regular meditation results in extraordinary improvements in compassion, kindness, and a more profound level of awareness.

Your Subconscious: The Power of Mental and Emotional Healing

We have arrived at a critical point in the history of humankind. An overwhelming amount of mental illness afflicts people the world over. These issues are frequently connected to criminality, therefore we should be especially cautious when assessing and managing mental health issues. The psychiatric profession alone cannot solve the mental health crises. In fact, this is not possible until society is prepared to accept and respond to the necessity of achieving healthy lifestyles, and understands the need to dismantle the insatiable lust for material goods and violence. Problems that arise in connection with managing emotions appear to be escalating. Divorces are often undertaken due to personal issues that have no root in emotions. We can see insane fears of problems with no basis in reality.

Recognizing the truth, the subconscious is often taught by repetition. Think about this repetition as someone chanting prayers regularly. Maintaining a sense of control over the mind is equally important to keeping an eye on the physical aspects. The body can require alcohol or sex; however, the mind is aware of the boundaries.

A sound body is the goal of the body-mind connection, bring him in a state of harmony. With a powerful unconscious and a set of strong beliefs, fundamental values, feelings, and connections associated with specific items, people, places, and ideas, we are in a position to dominate the world. Instead of falling victim to troublesome habits, let us look for new horizons and re-organize our minds like a computer would when optimized. If we can all learn to develop the subconscious and our emotions, our bodies will heal from the many pressures they are subjected to. Body language can be a clear reflection of the state of mind in which we are in—but the body must discover how to connect with the world around us if it is to take on the world.

a. The Act of Forgiving

Can we forgive ourselves?

As all of us know, forgiveness is a God-given quality. It is something we all want and strive to be able to demonstrate.

Bloodshed and violence are examples of situations in the past where forgiveness was not feasible, and mercy could not be shown due to ongoing tensions and hateful feelings about religious, communal, and caste issues. However, even in minor matters, such as errors made in disciplining children in their homes or at school, the issue of pardon is raised. In such cases, the parent or teacher has the power to accept forgiveness. Some may not be able to do so due to deep-rooted reasons, whereas others can without any problem. The media is filled with violent and vicious revenge stories over seemingly small injustices. This has become the subject of countless shows, films, and books we have all seen or read.

However, whatever wrongs are committed, forgiveness is offered at the end of the day because God is kind enough to forgive all transgressions. The spiritual side of us understands this divine justice. Penalties could be similar to punishments at school. However, the ability to accept forgiveness without a trace of anger and remove any negative feelings that might have arisen is a skill we must master. It is certainly not easy. Resolving minor, let alone major, annoyances with no grudges and saying "yes" without any hatred or disdain is holy in itself. However, attaining a deeper understanding of the briefness of our existence can aid in developing such unique feelings toward all living beings.

Additionally, we must understand that many errors in judgment occur because of personal human struggles. Crimes are not always committed with intention, but rather because a criminal is driven by situations that leave them with no other choice. They are left with their back against the wall. Although, in some cases, it may simply be out of greed that criminal activity occurs.

b. Removing Fear

We live in a world of fear. Perhaps it is true that the biggest fear we have as human beings is death. Even religion can be scary. Many of us are exposed to religious doctrine from a young age, imagining hell as the final destination for those who do something wrong. Children are taught to be scared of their minds from the beginning. Even the Constitution and our laws can cause fear through the power of ideas and strong language. Even the very subject of history can fill the human mind with worry. Films that aim to entertain us can also pose disturbing questions. However, individuals struggle to continue down the highway known as life amidst this all-encompassing fear.

We are all well aware that a minor injury could happen at any moment in our lives—during athletic games, travel, working with machines, on roller coasters, while boating, and even climbing trees. Indeed, every tiny, everyday activity could potentially fill us with fear. While a few of these are unavoidable, we are all too stoic against these little anxieties. Nevertheless, we cannot take everything for granted, as things can are not always as they seem. While the media may have us think otherwise, something as catastrophic as the disappearance of the Malaysian Airlines plane rarely happens. In this day and age, we require some confidence and positive thinking to overcome the irrational fear that has been instilled in our daily lives and routines. Prayers regularly remind us of the higher energy in our lives that connects the things that go wrong, even when what happens is the result of destiny.

Parents, seniors, preachers, and teachers could help humanity overcome the psychosis of fear. The practices of hypnosis and meditation could aid in overcoming humanity's most deeply-rooted and widespread fears. Phobias are specific fears, such as the fear of insects. With a well-planned daily routine of study, work, and play, no worry will be experienced once everything is in order. What happens if the bus does not show up or is in an accident? The entire world is seemingly thrown into a state of chaos and anxiety, or terror will temporarily take over the mind until the situation returns to normal. Instead of this reaction, we ought to conquer obstacles and hold our heads up. There is no reason to worry about law-abiding citizens with patriotic values and positive social beliefs. Every one of us will, at some point, likely require an attorney, a policeman, and a doctor to make sure we have a good life. In the meantime, let us work.

Try to feel safe. Remove the fear.

c. Freeing Your Mind

We are all born free but easily become entangled in chains soon after. The chains we are referring to, metaphorically, are the countless rules and restrictions we encounter in a world that aims to control us. Every organization has its own set of rules, a code of conduct, guidelines, and even a dress code. In the same way, the mind appears to be in a state of slavery out of habit from having free choice taken away.

If the mind is not allowed the freedom to develop without restraint, it will function more and more like an old machine that is rarely ever used nor maintained. It is necessary to engage in intense action to strengthen the mind, just as physical exercises strengthen the body. The scientific evidence behind the power of meditation has revealed that it can benefit the brain's functions. If we let our minds expand and bloom like the physical body can and will, our lives would be ablaze with an extraordinary glow. We would feel just as the captive colonies would have felt upon experiencing a taste of freedom. This feeling occurs when the mind seeks to reach a higher level. However, just like water needs an appropriately vast container such as the oceans, our minds need room to flex and grow.

Eliminate barriers and restrictions placed on the mind. Removing prejudices, blind hatred, anger, jealousy, and envy is part of letting the mind be genuinely free. If we see the mind as a well-maintained flower garden or an orchid of vibrant colors, that is what the ideal state of mind ought to be—a space where peace and joy can reside. Develop a mindset that sees the vastness of the sky and believes that all of humanity is one magnificent family unit in which no walls are in place. Perhaps the nature-based TV stations could assist in this endeavor. When we are exposed to nature's beauty first-hand, we naturally become more connected to the awareness of the vastness in which we play a significant role simply by being ourselves and becoming free.

HOW YOUR MIND WORKS

You are a human being, and while you were born with a mind present, you must take the time to learn how to use it best. There exist two different levels in your mind: the rational or conscious level and the subconscious or irrational one. You are the consciousness in your mind. Whatever you think about regularly sinks in through your subconscious brain, where it produces what you think in your conscious mind. This is where you store all of your thoughts and emotions. It is your creative mind. If you think positively, it will lead to good. If you have primarily evil thoughts and ideas, then evil will follow. This is how your mind operates. The primary thing to consider is that once the subconscious mind is convinced that an idea is valid, it will implement it. It is fascinating that the subconscious mind's law can be applied to both good and bad thoughts alike. If this law is used negatively, it will result in frustration, disappointment, and discontent in your life. However, when your daily thoughts are positive, harmonious, and in perfect balance, you will experience prosperity, success, and happiness.

The peace of your mind and the health of your body is inevitable once you begin to think and feel the correct way—positively. Whatever you say mentally and believe to be true will be manifested by your mind's subconscious, becoming the reality of your life. All that's required is to convince the subconscious to believe that your subconscious mind's ideas and laws will manifest the peace, health, or place you wish to be. Trust that if you make a command, your subconscious mind will faithfully repeat the thought you have imposed upon it. The rule of your mind causes it to receive a response or reaction to your unconscious mind based on whatever idea or thought you have within your mind's conscious.

Psychologists and psychiatrists say that impressions are formed within brain cells when thoughts are transmitted through your mind's subconscious. Once your subconscious takes in any thought and begins to implement it into action, it immediately generates the output of a combination of thoughts using all the knowledge you have acquired in your life to achieve the goal of that thought or action. It taps into the endless potential, energy, and wisdom within you. It combines the laws of nature to find its own way. Sometimes, this may lead you to a quick solution to your issues; however, in other instances, it could require weeks, days, or even longer. . . The power of the mind continues to have its mysteries.

DIFFERENTIATING BETWEEN THE CONSCIOUS AND SUBCONSCIOUS

It is important to remember that the conscious and subconscious are not two separate minds but two spheres of activity within one mind. The conscious part of your mind functions as your thinking mind. It is the part that makes choices. You can choose, for instance, what books to read, the place in which you reside, as well as who will be your partner. You make your choices by using your conscious mind. However, with no conscious thought on your part, the heart keeps beating, as do the entire processes of digestion, blood circulation, and respiration. These activities are carried out by your subconscious mind, which runs the processes that are not under your control.

The subconscious mind can accept what is impressed upon it or the beliefs you hold. However, it cannot think things through the way your conscious mind does and will not contest your beliefs with any form of debate. Your subconscious mind functions like the soil—open to any seeds, whether good or bad. Your thoughts are in motion and can be compared to seeds. Negative thoughts will remain in destructive thought patterns within your subconscious mind and, over time, will manifest into an outer reality that reflects this negativity.

Your subconscious mind is not involved in proving that your thoughts are positive or negative or whether they are true or untrue; however, it reacts to the character of your ideas or thoughts. For instance, if you think something is true, even though it may not be so, your subconscious mind will consider it true, generating results that naturally follow because you consciously believed in its truth.

EXPERIMENTS BY PSYCHOLOGISTS

Numerous studies conducted by psychologists and other experts on those in a state of hypnosis have demonstrated that our subconscious minds cannot make choices or perform the comparisons necessary to form a rational thought process. The results have repeatedly shown that the subconscious mind can and will accept any suggestion, no matter how false. After accepting all suggestions, your mind reacts to the suggestion's specifics. Showing the adaptability of the subconscious to the power of suggestion, a trained hypnotist may tell one of his clients he is Napoleon Bonaparte or even an animal of some kind. In response, the subject will play the character's role with uncanny precision. His character is altered in the meantime. He believes whatever the operator tells him is true about himself.

A skilled hypnotist might tell one pupil that their back is aching while in a state of hypnosis. He may inform another student that his nose is bleeding or that he is an ethereal statue. Perhaps he will tell one that he is frozen and that the temperature in the room is zero degrees. Each student will follow the specifics of his own assigned idea, utterly unaware of everything around him that does not support that particular idea. These easy illustrations show the difference between your thinking mentality and unconscious mind, which is not personal, non-selective, and accepts what you believe as truth. This, therefore, highlights the importance of choosing positive thoughts, ideas, uplifting concepts, and focusing on healing, inspiring, and filling your soul with happiness.

CLARIFICATION OF THE TERMS OBJECTIVE AND SUBJECTIVE MIND

Your conscious mind may also be called your objective mind, as it is concerned with objects outside. The objective mind is aware of the external world. It uses the five senses to observe one's environment and acquire knowledge. Your objective mind acts as your director and guide to understanding and experiencing your surroundings. Your mind's objective is educated through experience, observation, and education. As we have previously mentioned, the most crucial purpose of the objective mind is the ability to reason. Suppose you were one of the many visitors who travel to Los Angeles annually. You would take it all in through your objective mind and conclude that it is a stunning city based on your observations of parks, beautiful gardens, stunning buildings, and breathtaking houses. This is what happens when you are using your mind's objective view.

In contrast, your subconscious, or subjective, mind is often referred to as the emotional brain. Your subjective mind makes sense of its surroundings without employing your five senses. Instead, it interprets the world using the sense of intuition. It is the source of your emotions and also the repository of memories. The subjective mind can perform at its highest ability when your senses are not in a state of alertness. In simple terms, it is the intelligence manifested when your objective mind is in a sleepy or drowsy state. Your emotional brain sees things without the aid of your eyes. It can be described as having clairvoyance as well as hearing. The subjective mind can depart from your body, journey to far-off lands, and return with information that is usually of a most precise and authentic nature. With your subjective mind, you can discern other people's thoughts and examine what is inside sealed envelopes and closed safes. Your subjective mind can comprehend other people's thoughts without relying on usual methods of communication, such as writing or speech. It is critical to understand the relationship between the subjective and objective mind to master the art of praying.

WHY IS THE SUBCONSCIOUS UNABLE TO REASON LIKE THE CONSCIOUS MIND?

Your subconscious mind cannot be involved in debate. So, it follows that if you provide incorrect suggestions, it will accept these as truth and take them further to manifest them as circumstances, experiences, and even events. Every event in your life has resulted from the thoughts etched into your subconscious mind via beliefs. If you have conveyed false ideas in your unconscious mind, the only way to defeat them is to repeat positive, harmonious thoughts. Through this effort, your subconscious mind will take in these thoughts creating new, healthy habits of thinking and living.

The habitual, or most frequent, thoughts of your mind will create deep grooves within your subconscious, which is extremely favorable for you if those recurring thoughts are peaceful, harmonious, and constructive. However, if you have been a victim of fear, anxiety, and other negative thoughts, the solution is to realize the power of your unconscious mind. You can declare happiness, freedom, and total health. The subconscious, which is inventive and in tune with the divine source, will begin to bring about the joy and freedom you have proclaimed.

THE TREMENDOUS POWER OF SUGGESTION

Your conscious brain acts as a critically important "watchman at the gate," and its main job is to shield your mind's subconscious against false perceptions. You now know one of the most fundamental rules of the mind: your subconscious mind can accept suggestions. You now also know that your subconscious mind does not create comparisons or even contrasts, nor does it think or reason on its own as your conscious brain performs this function. Instead, it reacts only to perceptions presented to your mind by the conscious. It does not display opinions about one course of action over another.

The following is an excellent example of the incredible potential of the power suggestion. Imagine approaching a shy-looking passenger aboard a ship and telling the passenger, "You look extremely ill. What a pale face! You look like you are about to be ill right here. I will help you reach your cabin." The person immediately becomes pale and sickly looking. The suggestion of seasickness alone ties into his fears and trepidations. Your negative direction is realized. He becomes seasick, spending the next several hours feeling ill.

DIFFERENT REACTIONS TO THE SAME SUGGESTION

People react in various ways to the same idea due to their unconscious beliefs or conditioning. For instance, if you visit a sailor on a ship and sympathetically inform him, "My dear fellow, you're looking ill. Are you feeling sick? You look as if you are seasick," the sailor will probably laugh at you. Or, perhaps he will express mild irritation over the suggestion that one who spends a lifetime at sea could potentially be seasick. Your comment about seasickness did not go over well, in this case, because in his mind, he was immune to it. To the sailer, your suggestion was laughable and brought up feelings of self-confidence instead of fear, leading to a very different type of response.

According to the dictionary, an act of suggestion is putting something in one's mind, or the mental process that takes place when the thought or concept that is suggested is accepted, entertained and then implemented. Remember that a suggestion cannot be imposed on the subconscious mind against the wishes of the conscious mind. That is, your conscious mind can deny requests. In the scenario of the seaman, the sailor was not worried about seasickness. He was convinced of his health, and therefore any negative thought could not incite anxiety. However, the idea of seasickness being mentioned to the passenger triggered an underlying fear that he always had. Everyone has their thoughts, fears, and beliefs and these assumptions guide our lives. The power of a suggestion is not inherently going to affect someone, except when that person believes it. Your subconscious powers are triggered to operate in a restricted and limited manner based on a particular idea.

HOW HE LOST HIS ARM

A friend of mine presents a series of talks at the London Truth Forum in Caxton Hall. He established this forum several years ago. It was co-founded by Dr. Evelyn Fleet, the director of the Forum. She once informed him of an article in English newspapers that focused on how powerful suggestion can be. The article discussed a request that a man created in his mind over two years. "I would give my right arm to see my daughter cured," he had once said. It seemed that his daughter was suffering from a severe form of arthritis and incurable skin disease. Many medical treatments failed to treat the problem, and the father had felt an intense desire for his daughter to experience a full recovery. He expressed this desire by speaking those words.

Sometime after, the family was driving in their car when their vehicle collided with another. Dr. Fleet indicated that the father's left arm was cut off at the shoulder. Almost immediately after, the daughter's skin issues and arthritis completely disappeared. With this in mind, you should always be sure to provide your subconscious with only suggestions that help, bless, lift, and encourage you in all ways. Your subconscious is not able to make jokes. It will take your words at face value.

HOW AUTOSUGGESTION BANISHES FEAR

In its various forms, autosuggestion is the act of expressing something specific to oneself. In an excellent guide to autosuggestion, Herbert Parkyn documents an incident. It is funny, which is why one can so easily remember it.

A New York visitor in Chicago is looking at his watch, set to New York time, one hour in advance of a Chicago clock. He informs a Chicago acquaintance that it is noon. Unaware of the time difference between Chicago and New York, the Chicago friend tells the New Yorker that he is suddenly ravenous and needs to take lunch.

Autosuggestion can be used to alleviate various anxieties and other negative circumstances. Here is an example. A young singer was asked to audition for a role. She was excited about the audition; however, she had failed three times previously, likely because she was afraid of failing. This girl had an incredible voice; however, she kept telling herself, "When it comes time for me to perform, what if they don't enjoy my voice? I am overwhelmed by anxiety and fear." The unconscious mind accepted these autosuggestions as a demand and began to manifest them, bringing them into her life. The root of the problem was not her voice but involuntary autosuggestion that occurred when unconscious fears became emotionalized and subjectified.

The story has a happy ending. The singer overcame the autosuggestions by using the following method three times per day. She confined herself to an area, settled down in an armchair, relaxed her body, and shut her eyes. She slowed her body and mind as best as she could. Physical inertia can increase mental vigilance and make the mind more open to suggestions. She responded to the suggestion of fear by telling herself, "I perform beautifully. I am poised, confident, calm, and relaxed." Then, she repeated this mantra slowly, calmly, and with a sense of purpose five to ten times every session. She attended three "sittings" every day and another before bed. After one week, she was at ease and felt confident. When the opportunity to audition came again, she gave an amazing, incredible audition.

HOW SHE RESTORED HER MEMORY
A seventy-five-year-old woman was habitually declaring to herself, "I am losing my memory." She reverted the practice

when she realized it and used an autosuggestion that she induced several times per day. She stated, "My memory today has improved in all aspects. I will always remember everything I must know at any given time and at every point of space. The impressions I receive will be more specific. They will be retained automatically and effortlessly. What I need to remember will instantly appear in the proper form in my brain. I am getting better every day, and shortly, the memory of my brain will become sharper than ever before." After three weeks, her memory returned to normal, and she was thrilled.

HOW HE OVERCAME A NASTY TEMPER

Many people who complain of anger issues and bad tempers turn out to be extremely vulnerable to autosuggestion, which is impacting their lives negatively. They can achieve excellent results simply by using these statements at least three times per day—at noon, morning, and before going to sleep—for about one month. "Henceforth, I will become more jovial. Joy, happiness, and cheeriness are becoming my normal mind. Each day, I am becoming more loved and more understanding. I am now the epicenter of happiness and goodwill to everyone around me and am transforming them into a source of positive humor. This joyful, happy, and positive state of mind is becoming my usual, default mental state. I am grateful." It is quite effective.

THE CONSTRUCTIVE AND DESTRUCTIVE POWER OF SUGGESTION

Now, for a few illustrations and remarks on heterosuggestion. Heterosuggestions are suggestions made by another person. The ability to suggest has played an integral role in the lives and thoughts of mankind throughout history and across the globe. In many regions, it is the dominant force in religion. The suggestion provides a method to control and discipline us, but it could also be employed to gain control over those who are not aware of the rules of the mind. In its positive form, it is amazing and beautiful. However, in its negative aspect, it is among the most damaging of response patterns of the mind. It results in repeated patterns of suffering, sickness, and catastrophe.

HAVE YOU ACCEPTED ANY OF THESE?
From the beginning, humans receive a great deal of harmful advice. We unknowingly took them as gospel without any real and effective way to combat these suggestions.

Here are a few negative thoughts that seem to surface in our lives repeatedly: "You cannot." "You will never make a difference." "You must not." "You will fall short." "You will never have the opportunity." "You are incorrect." "It is useless." "It is not about what you know, but who you know." "The world is going to the dogs." "What's the point? Is there any value? Nobody cares." "It is not worth trying to do it all over again." "You"re way too old for this now." "Things only continue to get more dire." "Life is a never-ending struggle." "You just cannot beat them." "You will be in debt." "You will get the virus." "You cannot trust any heart."

Unless you are an adult who employs constructive auto-suggestion as a reconditioning treatment, the impressions you received in the past may cause patterns that lead to problems in your personal and social life. Autosuggestion helps to free your mind from the burden of negative mental habits that could otherwise alter your behavior patterns, hindering the development of positive habits.

YOU CAN COUNTERACT NEGATIVE SUGGESTIONS

Go through the newspaper on any day, and you are sure to come across various articles that can plant seeds of insanity, fear, anxiety, or that indicate the imminent end-of-the-world. If you allow these ideas to be accepted by your mind, the fear could lead to a loss of motivation to live. Be aware that you can reject any negative suggestion by offering your subconscious mind positive auto-suggestions in its place. You can thwart destructive thoughts. Make sure you are aware of any negative advice people offer to you. The burden of being influenced by harmful heterosuggestion is not necessary. It can be avoided, even though everyone has experienced it in one way or another during youth and adolescence. If you think back, you will be able to recall how your parents, family members, teachers, and others contributed to the ongoing campaign of negative advice. Examine the messages they gave to you, and you will find that much of it was an attempt to spread propaganda. Of course, the primary purpose behind much of what was spoken was to manipulate or instill fear about the people around you. The heterosuggestion process is a constant throughout every office, home, factory, and club. Many of these suggestions create a mindset that makes you think, feel, and behave according to what others want and in ways that work to benefit them—rather than you.

HOW SUGGESTION KILLED A MAN

Here is an example of a dangerous heterosuggestion: A friend of mine visited a crystal gazer in India who informed him that he had a weak heart and would die at the next moon. He began to tell his entire family about the prediction and arranged his will. This thought-provoking suggestion sank deep into his subconscious, and the man accepted it with complete confidence. My friend also informed me that the crystal gazer was believed to have mysterious powers of the occult and could do good or harm to someone. He was a dead man by the next moon, but did not realize that he had been the cause of his own demise. Most of us have been told similar ridiculous, stupid tales of superstition.

Let us examine what happened in light of how the subconscious mind functions. Whatever the rational man's mind thinks, the subconscious mind accepts. My friend was content and active, healthy and strong when visiting the fortune-teller. She made a highly negative prediction that he accepted. He was terrified and would often think about the reality that he would die during the next moon. He then began to inform everybody that he would die soon and even made preparations for the day of his death. The event had already taken place in his mind because of his thoughts. Essentially, he caused his own"death," or at least the destruction of his physical body due to his trepidation and expectation of finality. His demise was "predicted" based on nothing more than sticks and stones laid on the ground. The fortune teller's idea was not powerful enough to bring about the outcome she predicted. If he had been aware of the laws of his mind, then he would have dismissed the suggestion as a negative and refused to pay her ideas any consideration. He would have known that he was controlled and guided only by his own thoughts and emotions. Like tin-based arrows directed at a warship, the prophecy of this crystal gazer could have been removed and neutralized without causing any harm.

The moral of this story is that other people's ideas do not have any authority over you other than the power you grant them through your thinking. You must signify your thoughts; you must entertain positive thoughts. They will soon turn into your habitual thoughts, and you will think about these good things more. Remember that you have the power to decide. Choose life! Choose love! Choose health!

THE POWER OF AN ASSUMED MAJOR PREMISE

Your mind functions as a syllogism, which means that whatever idea your conscious mind believes to be true determines the conclusion your subconscious comes to regarding a specific question or issue. If the premise you believe in is true, the conclusion must be valid. For example, each virtue is worthy of praise. Kindness is a virtue. Thus, kindness is a laudable attribute. Another example is the notion that everything is formed, changes, and eventually dies. The Pyramids of Egypt were formed; therefore, the Pyramids will disappear one day. The first sentence is called the main premise, and the correct conclusion must be based on the correct premise.

A college professor who attended a few of mind-science lectures in 1962 at Town Hall in New York once told, "Everything about my existence is a mess. I have lost my health, wealth, and even friends. Everything I do turns out wrong." He was advised to make a central premise of the thoughts that the inexhaustible intelligence of his subconscious mind directed and empowered both mentally and physically. In the future, his subconscious mind would automatically guide him with wisdom in connection with his investments and decision-making. It would also recover his body and restore his mind to peace and harmony.

The professor followed the advice and came up with an overall vision of how he would like his life to go. This was the primary premise of his work: "Infinite intelligence guides and leads me through all my paths. My perfect health is mine, as my body is healthy, and the Law of Harmony operates in my body and mind. Peace, beauty, love, and prosperity are my own. The concept of righteous action and divine law govern my life. I am aware that my main base is on the timeless facts of life. I feel, know, and trust that the subconscious brain acts out my conscious mind's thoughts."

He wrote to me as follows: "I repeated the above statements slowly and with love several times throughout the day, knowing that they were sinking deeper into my subconscious mind and that results would follow. Thanks to the opportunity you provided by guiding me, all areas of my life have changed for the better. It is working!"

THE SUBCONSCIOUS DOES NOT ARGUE

Your mind's subconscious is intelligent and has answers to every question. It will not disagree with you or speak in your direction. As an example, if you tell yourself, "I cannot do this," or, "I am too old," or, "I cannot fulfill these obligations," or, "I do not know the right person," you are infusing your mind with these negative thoughts, and it will respond in kind. This prevents you from doing your best and creates a lack of control and a sense of anger in your life. If you create obstacles or delays in your mind, you deny the wisdom and insight that reside within the subconscious brain. You are, in essence, telling yourself that the subconscious cannot solve the problem. It can lead to emotional and mental congestion, illness, and even psychotic tendencies. To fulfill your dreams and to overcome your anger, recite this powerful affirmation at least once a day:

"The infinite intelligence that gave me this desire directs, guides, and then reveals the best method for achieving my dream. I recognize the greater intuition in my unconscious reacting. I know that what I experience and believe within is manifested by the outside. There is balance in equilibrium and peace."

If you tell yourself, "There is no way out; I am lost; there is no way out of this dilemma; I am stymied and blocked," you will get no response or answer from your unconscious mind. If you would like your subconscious to help you, send it the proper request to obtain its cooperation. It is continually working to your benefit. It controls the pace of your heart right now as well as your breathing. It can heal a wound on your finger. Moreover, it constantly looks after your health and keeps you safe and well. However, your subconscious mind has an individual mind connected; it will accept your thoughts and images.

When seeking an answer to a query, the subconscious mind will react. However, it expects you to first make an accurate judgment within your mind's eye. It is essential to acknowledge that the answer lies in the subconscious of your mind. If you think, "I do not think there is a way out. I am confused. Why do not I receive answers?" then you will still the wheels of your mind. Instead, let them go and let it go. Simply remain quiet and declare, "My subconscious knows the answer. It is now responding to me. Thank you for the fact that the inexhaustible wisdom of my subconscious is aware of everything and is providing the right answer for me right now. My true conviction is liberating the power and splendor of my unconscious mind. I am glad that it is that way."

REVIEW OF HIGHLIGHTS

Think of the good, and good will follow. Consider wrong, and then, evil will be the result. What do you think about throughout the day? Your subconscious mind does not fight with you. It follows what your conscious mind dictates. If you think, "I cannot afford it," it may be accurate, but do not declare it. Find a more positive thought and decide, "I'll buy it soon. I will accept the idea in my mind." You are in control of your own choices. Pick happiness and health. You can choose to be a friendly person or to be unfriendly. If you choose to be joyful, cooperative, and lovable, the world will react positively. This is the most effective way to create a beautiful personality.

The conscious part of your mind acts as your "watchman at the gate." Its primary job is to guard the subconscious against false beliefs. You can choose to believe that something wonderful will happen and is taking place right now. Your greatest strength is the ability to make choices. Choose to be happy and abundant. The words and opinions of others are not able to harm you. Only you have the power to think for yourself. You can choose to disapprove of the words or opinions of others and believe in that which is good. You are in control of the way you respond. Be careful what you say. You are accountable for every idle sentence. Do not ever declare, "I will fail," or, "I will lose my job," or, "I cannot pay my rent." Your subconscious cannot accept an opportunity to laugh. It, instead, brings everything to fruition.

Your mind is not an evil thing. The forces of nature are not hostile. It is all about how you utilize the power of nature. Use your mind to heal, bless, and motivate all those around you.

Never say, "I cannot." You must be able to overcome your fear by substituting the following statement: "I can do anything with the help of my own mind's subconscious." Consider thinking from the perspective of timeless wisdom and fundamentals of the world rather than from the viewpoint of ignorance, fear, and structured belief systems. Do not let others control your thinking. Instead, pick your ideas and make your own choices. You are the master of your soul (subconscious brain) and the one who decides your destiny. Remember that you have the power to make a choice. Choose life! Choose love! Choose health! Choose happiness! Whatever your conscious mind believes to be real, your subconscious mind will take as fact and manifest it. Believe in luck, God's guidance, divine wisdom, completing the right actions, and all blessings that come with life.

MENTAL HEALING IN MODERN TIMES

These days, everyone is concerned about effectively treating ailments in the physical body and those that impact mental health. What exactly is healing, though? Where does the power to heal come from? This is the ever-present question that has long been asked by humankind. Answer: healing power comes from the subconscious brain of every person. A change in the mental attitude of the person suffering can activate this healing power, even if no religious figure, psychiatrist, psychologist, scientist, or medical professional has ever treated the patient.

The doctor dresses the wound. The psychologist or psychiatrist then proceeds to eliminate the mental blockages within the patient to release the healing principle and restore the patient to health. The surgeon removes the physical obstruction, allowing healing energy to function as it should. The surgeon, doctor, or cognitive science professional will claim that they each healed the patient. However, they only played a minor role. The truest healing power is identified by various names, such as nature, life, God, creative intelligence, and subconscious power. As previously mentioned, there are multiple ways to eliminate the emotional, mental, and physical barriers that block the flow of healing life-principle that runs through every one of us. The healing principle within your subconscious mind can and will cleanse your body and mind of all diseases if directed by you or another person. The healing principle works across all human beings, regardless of religion or color. It is not necessary to be a member of a particular church to participate in the healing process. Your subconscious will be able to heal the wound or burn on your hand, even if you claim to be an atheist or an agnostic.

Current psychotherapy procedures rely on the inexhaustible ability and wisdom within the subconscious brain and, often, its connection to a person's faith. The practitioner of mental sciences or minister adheres to the instruction from the training or the Bible, i.e., entering the room and closing the door, enabling a strong focus of mind and a deep state of relaxation. Then, they allow the individual to speak while thinking about the infinite healing power within the person. The practitioner closes the doors to his mind from any external distractions and the world around him, then silently and with a smile, turns over the issue or thought to his subconscious mind, realizing that the mind will respond to his particular needs. The most amazing thing you can learn is to imagine a goal you want to achieve and feel its realness. Then, the eternal life force will react to your request, and it will be granted. This is the process a modern-day mental scientist undergoes when practicing prayer therapy.

ONE PROCESS OF HEALING

The universal principle of healing runs deep within all things. It is the unifying power between everything: the cat, dog, tree, grass, wind, and earth, for everything is alive. This principle of life is operative through the vegetable, animal, and mineral kingdoms through an instinct and the principle of development. Humanity is conscious of this principle of life and can influence it to consciously benefit in many ways. There are numerous methods and approaches to harnessing the power of all beings. However, there is only one method of healing: faith. According to your faith, this healing will be performed on you.

THE LAW OF BELIEF

The world's religions provide a wide variety of beliefs, explained in various ways. The very basis of life is the belief system. A belief system includes your own particular answers to questions such as: What do you think about yourself, your life, or the entire universe? What happens to you is in part based on what you believe. Belief is made up of thoughts, and as you think about them, it creates the power of your subconscious, which is spread throughout all aspects of your life.

Realize that when we refer to faith, it is not the faith the Bible speaks about in terms of ceremony, ritual, form, institution, or any specific formula for religion. Faith is, instead, about the concept of belief. Your own belief is truly as simple as the thoughts that occupy your mind. If you believe that everything is possible for him who believes (MARK 9:23), then the wrong thing to do is trust that something will cause harm. Keep in mind that it is not the thing you believe in that has the power to harm or hurt you, but the thought that you have in your head that causes the effect. Your experiences, actions, and every event and circumstance you encounter reflect and react to the thoughts within your mind.

The Ice Mountain

Mind Model

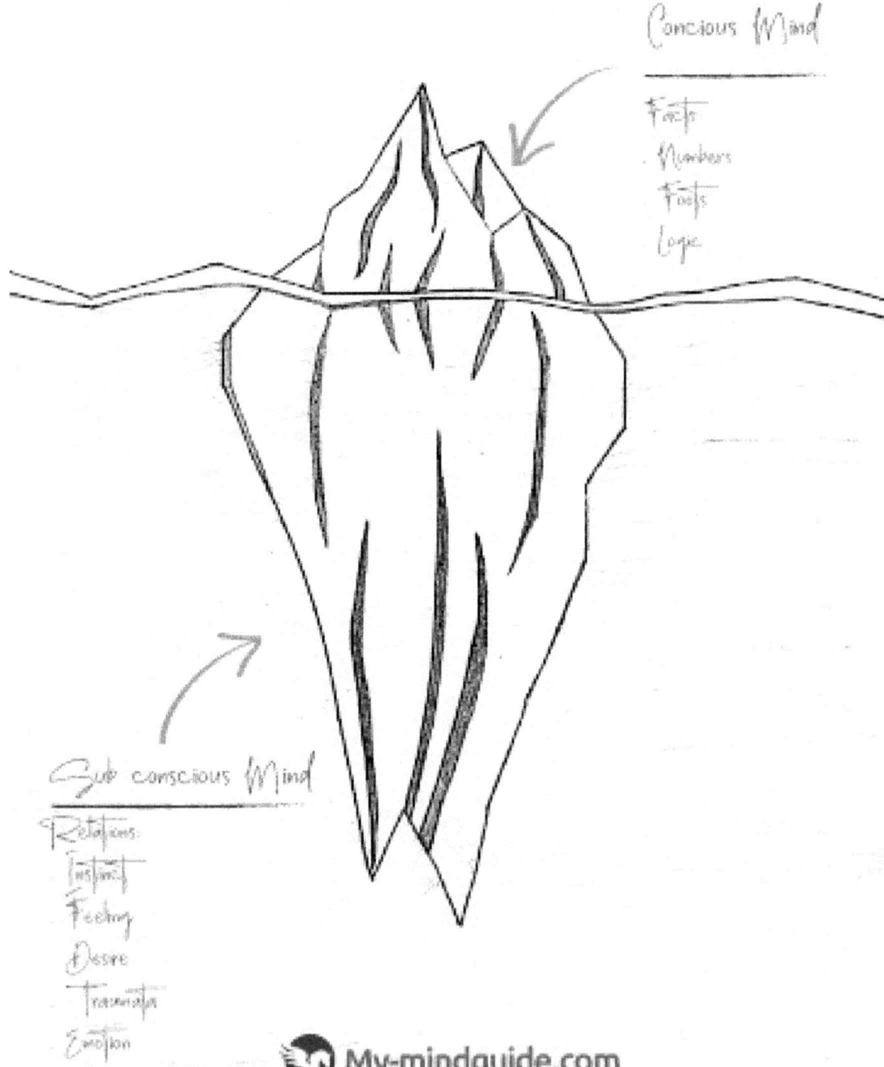

PRAYER THERAPY

THE SCIENTIFICALLY-DIRECTED SUBCONSCIOUS MIND

The practice of prayer is the synchronized, efficient, and intelligent operation of the subconscious and conscious levels of the mind so that they are specifically targeted toward a specific goal. When you engage in scientific prayer or prayer therapy, you need to know the purpose of your practice and why you are doing it. You must trust the law of healing. Prayer therapy can be called mental therapy as well as scientific prayer. In the practice of prayer, you can select a specific idea or mental image that you want to feel. You recognize your ability to transmit this idea or picture to the subconscious by experiencing your actual situation. When you remain committed to your mind, the prayer you have made can be fulfilled. The practice of prayer is a specific mental activity with a specific goal.

Let us suppose you decide to get rid of a specific issue by using prayer therapy. You know that your illness or problem, regardless of what it may be, is due to negative thoughts fueled by fear ingrained in your subconscious mind. You are also aware that you will receive healing if you succeed in removing these thoughts from your mind. Therefore, it is advisable to look to the healing power in your subconscious mind to unlock its unending potential, wisdom, and ability to heal any circumstances. When you meditate on these facts, the fear you have will diminish, and the remainder of these truths will also help correct the false belief systems. You should express gratitude for the healing you believe will happen. After the prayer, you should try to keep your thoughts off the problem until you are guided by a time to repeat your prayer. When you pray, you must employ an absolute refusal to acknowledge for even a second that healing is not coming. This mental attitude creates harmony between the subconscious and conscious mind, which activates the energy necessary for healing.

FAITH HEALING AND HOW BLIND FAITH WORKS

Faith healing is not connected to the type of religion mentioned in the Bible but rather to the relationship between the subconscious and conscious mind. A faith healer heals with no knowledge of the power and forces at work. He could declare that he has an innate ability to heal, and therefore the patient's faith in his abilities results in positive results. The voodoo physicians across South Africa and other parts of the globe seemingly cure their patients through incantations, touching the saints' bones, or any other cure method. As long as it causes the patient to trust the technique or procedure, it can heal their ailment. Any approach that allows individuals to shift their thoughts from anxiety and fear to faith and optimism will help cure. Many people claim that since their belief system yields outcomes, it is the right one. As discussed in this section, it cannot be true.

To show how blind faith operates, we will discuss Swiss doctor Franz Anton Mesmer. In 1776, he announced various cures brought about by stroking patients' bodies with artificial magnets. In the years to follow, he demolished his magnets and developed the concept of animal magnetism. Mesmer believed that there was an underlying fluid that runs through the universe, but that is most present in the human body.

He stated that this magnetic fluid, flowing from his body to his patients, helped heal them. People came to him in great numbers to be healed, and many amazing cures were discovered. Mesmer relocated to Paris and, while he was there, the government set up a committee composed of doctors and members of the Academy of Science, of which Benjamin Franklin was a member, to investigate his cures. The report acknowledged the most important assertions made by Mesmer. Still, it concluded that there was no evidence to show the validity of his theory of magnetic fluid and that the results could be attributed to the imaginations of his patients.

After this was revealed, Mesmer was driven into exile until he passed away in 1815. The following year, Dr. Braid of Manchester attempted to prove that magnetic fluid did not have anything directly to do with the genesis of healings performed by Mesmer. Dr. Braid found that patients could be taken into a hypnotic state through suggestion, and during this time, several of the well-known phenomenon attributed to magnetism could be induced. Treatments were brought to fruition by the active mind of patients and the powerful belief in their own minds. This is one example of what could be described as blind faith since there was no comprehension of how these cures came into being.

SUBJECTIVE FAITH AND WHAT IT MEANS

It is a common belief that an individual's unconscious or subjective mind is capable of being controlled by his own objective or conscious mind, just as it is to someone else's ideas. Therefore, whatever might be your true conviction, if you have faith either actively or passively, your subconscious mind is controlled by suggestion, and your desires will be fulfilled. The faith required for mental healing is a subjective faith that is possible to attain upon the end of active resistance from the conscious or objective mind. In order to heal the body, it is vital to have the simultaneous trust of both the subconscious and conscious mind. It is also helpful to enter an ethereal state and receptivity by relaxing the body and mind and falling asleep. In this state of drowsiness, your body becomes more open to subjective perception.

I once received a question from a gentleman, asking, "How is it that I received a healing from the ministry of a priest? I did not believe the claims he made when he said that the word "disease" does not exist and that I have none." The man initially thought his intellect was being insulted. He protested this blatant absurdity. The reason he was healed was easy. He was slowed down by soothing words and instructed to remain in a still state, do nothing, and avoid thinking of anything for the moment. His pastor also sat passively and recited in quiet, tranquil, and continuous statements for approximately one-half hour, stating that the man would experience total health, peace, harmony, and completeness. He felt a tremendous sense of relief and did return to full health.

His faith in God was reflected in his inability to accept treatment, and the idea of achieving perfect health by the doctor was transmitted into his unconscious mind. Both of their minds were then in a relationship. Autosuggestions resulting from doubt about the healer's abilities or accuracy in the theories did not hinder the healer from the patient. In this drowsy, sleepy state, the conscious mind's resistance is decreased to a minimum, and the result is observed. If the suggestion controls the person's subconscious, it performs tasks in line with that suggestion and triggers a healing process.

THE MEANING OF ABSENT TREATMENT

Imagine that you suddenly found out your mother had been ill while at her home in New York City, but you resided in Los Angeles. Your mother would not be present physically where you are; however, you could still pray for her. It is God's Father who does the work. The law of creative thinking (subconscious mind) is there to help you and will perform the job effectively. The response, given your needs, is automatic. Your treatment has the purpose of creating an inner awareness of harmony and health in your mind. This inner awareness, operating via the unconscious mind, is a result of the subconscious mind of your mother, as there is only one creative mind. Your thoughts about wellness, vitality, and perfection run through this universal mind. It sets the course of the subjective side and manifests through the body as an act of healing.

According to the mind principle, there is no such thing as time or space. The same mind operates through your mother regardless of where she is located physically. There is no alternative to the present treatment because all reasons are always present. It is not your intention to express thoughts or think. Your approach is a conscious flow of your mind. As you begin to recognize the advantages of well-being, health, and relaxation, your characteristics will be revived by your mother's experience, and the results will be evident.

The following is an excellent example of effective treatment. Recently, a participant on our radio show located in Los Angeles prayed for her mother in New York who had experienced a coronary thrombosis. She said, "The healer is exactly in the place where she is. The physical condition reflects her lifestyle as shadows cast onto the screen. I am aware that I have to alter the projector reel to change the image on the screen. The projection reel is my mind, and I am now projecting the images of harmony, peace, and total health for my mother. The infinite healing force that created my mother's body and all of her organs now fills every atom in her body. A stream of peace runs through every cell of her body. Doctors are guided by God and directed. Anyone who has contact with my mother will be guided to follow the correct path. I am aware that illness is not a reality in itself. If it were, none of us would be cured. I am now in alignment with the eternal principle of love and life. I am convinced that peace and harmony are currently manifesting within my mother's physical body."

She prayed in this way several times a day, and her mother made an astonishing recovery within a couple of days, to the delight of her doctor. He was impressed by her faith based on God's strength. The conclusion reached by the daughter's mind put the creative law of mind to work in the subjective aspect of life. It manifested through the appearance of her mother's body as being in perfect wellness and balance. The daughter's feelings towards her mother were brought back to life by her mother.

3 Main Forms of Hypnotherapy

KINETIC ACTION OF THE SUBCONSCIOUS MIND

A psychologist informed me that his lung was affected by an ailment. The X-rays and the analysis revealed tuberculosis was present. Before going to bed, he would reaffirm, "Every cell of my body, nerve, tissue, and muscle in my lungs are becoming completely clean, pure, and flawless. My entire body is returning to harmony, health, and balance." While they are not the exact words he used, they are the essence of what he believed. In response, the complete healing occurred within one month. Later, X-rays confirmed this perfect and flawless healing. I was curious about his method, so I asked him why he would repeat the same words before bed.

In response, he told me, "The motion in the unconscious mind goes on throughout your sleep time. Therefore, you should give your subconscious mind something to think about as you fall asleep." It was an extremely wise rationale.

When thinking of peace and health, the man never spoke of his problems by name. I strongly suggest you stop talking about your problems or giving them names and identities. The only source from which they get the attention of others is through your anxiety about them. As the psychologist mentioned above, you can develop into an expert in mental surgery. In the end, your problems will be cut away like dead branches being cut from trees. You block the kinetic process by constantly listing the symptoms and aches you experience. Therefore, you are not releasing the healing energy and power that your mind stores in your subconscious. In addition, according to the laws of your mind, your imaginings form into something that can be frightening. Infuse your mind with only the most profound facts of life, and then walk ahead in the light of love.

SUMMARY OF YOUR AIDS TO HEALTH

Find out what helps you. Recognize that correct guidance provided by your unconscious mind can restore your body and mind. Make a plan to fill your unconscious mind with your wants and needs. Imagine the desired outcome and experience its actuality. If you follow the plan, you will see results.

- Choose what you believe. Be aware that belief is made up of the thoughts that you create in your head.

- It is not wise to believe in the possibility of illness or something that can cause general harm or harm you directly. Believe in perfect health, peace, prosperity, and divine guidance.

- The noble and great thoughts you tend to dwell on are amazing actions. Use the power of prayers in your daily life. Select a specific idea, concept, or mental image.

- Be emotionally and mentally connected to this idea. If you keep your mental state positive, your prayers will be granted.

- Remember, should you desire to heal the body, it is possible to attain it through faith. Faith is understanding the connection and functioning of your unconscious and conscious mind.

- Faith is the result of knowing.

- Blind faith is the term used to describe how one can see healing results without a science-based understanding of the powers or forces at work.

- Make it a habit to pray for loved ones who might be suffering. Be quiet in your prayers, and your thoughts about vitality, health, and perfection, which run through the mind of all people, will be felt within the mind of the person you love dearly.

USE YOUR SUBCONSCIOUS MIND TO REMOVE FEAR

Once, a student informed me that he had been asked to speak at a dinner. He admitted to being terrified at the prospect of speaking in front of 1,000 people. In response, he fought back his anxiety in this manner: For a few nights, he would sit in an armchair and try to relax his mind. For around five minutes, he told himself slowly, calmly, and with conviction, "I am going to overcome this anxiety. I am overcoming it today. I can speak with confidence and poise. I am relaxed and comfortable." By following an unquestionable law of mind, he conquered his fears.

The subconscious mind is open to suggestions and guided by those suggestions. When you let your mind go free, the thoughts you have are absorbed into your subconscious via a process similar to osmosis, in which a porous membrane separates two fluids. When positive thoughts enter the unconscious and grow, they can grow and you can become calm, peaceful, tranquil, and calm.

MAN'S GREATEST ENEMY

The saying goes that the fear of death is man's most formidable foe. Fear is the cause of illness, death, and imperfect human relations. Many people are scared of the past while fearing the chaos and uncertainty of the future and their own potential death. Fear is any thought that passes through your mind and causes you to be afraid or fearful. Let's discuss this in greater detail. A child may be frightened when he thinks he hears a boogieman in his bedroom attempting to abduct him. However, when his father flicks on the lights and informs him that there is no boogieman, he is liberated from any fear. The terror in the child's mind is as real and convincing *to him* as if there was indeed a boogieman or other fearsome creature present. However, he was cured of an untrue thought within his head. His fear was not real as it was not based on a true thought. Similarly, most of our own fears do not have a basis in reality. They are merely an array of dark shadows that appear frightening… but the shadows are not really what they seem.

DO THE THING YOU FEAR

Ralph Waldo Emerson, philosopher and poet, once said, "Do the thing you are afraid to do, and the death of fear is certain." There was a time when the writer in this article was afflicted with utter fear of facing an audience. However, he overcame that fear by standing in front of the audience and doing precisely what he was afraid of doing. Then, the end of fear was guaranteed. If you declare that you will conquer your fears and make a definitive choice to do so in your conscious mind, you are releasing the power of your subconscious mind, which flows depending on how you frame your thinking. You are conquering your fear.

BANISHING STAGE FRIGHT

You may recall that we earlier discussed a young singer who had been invited for an audition. She was excited about the audition. However, despite having an incredible singing voice, she had not performed well on three prior occasions due to stage fright. The woman was so sure that she would experience fear of the stag when it was time to sing that she caused her own failures.

The subconscious mind accepts your fears as a demand, then manifests these fears, bringing them into your life. Having sung the wrong notes in all three previous auditions, finally, she fell and wept. The root of the problem was, as we previously explained, an involuntary autosuggestion, i.e., a subconscious fear that was emotionally distorted and subjectified. You will remember that she overcame it by following a particular procedure three times daily. Sitting alone in an area, settled down in an armchair, she relaxed her body and shut her eyes. She calmed her body and mind to the highest of her abilities. Physical inertia encourages passiveness and makes the mind more open to suggestions. She countered the fear suggestion by repeatedly stating its opposite and telling herself, "I perform beautifully. I am poised, calm, relaxed, and confident."

She spoke these words slowly and calmly, repeating them up to ten times every sitting. She went through three "sittings" daily and an additional one right before bed. When she finished one week of these declarations, she appeared composed and confident and delivered an awe-inspiring performance. I urge you to perform the same procedure, modifying it as needed for your particular situation, and the end of fear is guaranteed.

FEAR OF FAILURE

Sometimes, students from local universities come to school teachers reporting that they suffer from amnesia-like symptoms during exams. The complaints are always similar: "I know the answers when the test is over. However, I cannot remember the answers while taking the test." The stated concept, which then manifests itself, is what we can always expect to occur in our lives. I have personally observed that everyone is obsessed with the notion of failing. This fear is the cause of this temporary amnesia and what causes the whole experience.

Let's look at a specific example. One medical student was the brightest in his class. However, the student could not answer basic writing or oral test questions correctly. He would become deeply worried for several days prior to the exam. The negative thoughts were infused with anxiety. His subconscious experienced these negative thoughts, encased in the intense emotion of fear. This young man was, essentially, repeatedly asking the subconscious to prove that he failed, which is what it did during each exam. Finally, the day after an exam, when he remembered all the answers to the questions, he discovered that he was suffering from a psychological state—apparent amnesia.

HOW HE OVERCAME THE FEAR

When he finally figured out the issues he was facing, he realized that to achieve his academic and career goals, he would have to overcome his fear of failure. He learned that the subconscious brain was the repository of memory and that it kept a complete recording of all the things he read and heard during his medical school experiences. Furthermore, he discovered that his subconscious mind was open to suggestion and that he would have to change the suggestions that were being presented.

He had to ensure he felt relaxed, at peace, calm, and confident to do so. To do this, he would imagine his mother congratulating him on his outstanding academic record or test scores each night and every morning. He would imagine a letter of academic honor held in her hand. As he began to consider these positive outcomes, he invoked a reaction within himself. The all-knowing and powerful subconscious power was in charge. It dictated and controlled his mind. He imagined the ending he desired by directing the path to achieve that goal. After this process, the student passed all of his subsequent tests. Also, his intuition was in control, enabling him to provide a dazzling outcome.

COMMON FEARS: WATER, MOUNTAINS, ENCLOSED PLACES, ETC.

Many common fears affect proportionately more people than others. Many human beings are afraid to get into an elevator, scale mountain ranges, look from high cliffs, or even swim in the sea. For some, this could be because they encountered bad experiences in their early years. For instance, being thrown forcefully into the ocean without knowing how to swim could lead someone to fear the sea. Also, it is possible that being forcibly locked in an elevator that did not function as it should could lead to anxiety about closed spaces.

I was once in a frightening situation at ten years old. I had unintentionally slipped into a pool of deep water and was swept through three sets of waterfalls. I remember the black water engulfing my head and being desperately breathless until a boy pulled me out at the very last moment. This incident sank deep into my unconscious mind, and I was terrified of water for a long time.

Then, an old psychologist advised me, "Go towards that pool, gaze at the water, and scream out in loud tones, 'I will conquer you. I will dominate you.' Then go into the water, and overcome it." This is precisely what I did, and I was able to master the water. There was no more fear. Do not allow water—or any other fear—to dominate you. Remember that you are the one who controls the fear. Once I adopted a different mindset, my powerful subconscious gave me strength, faith, and confidence, enabling me to conquer my fear.

MASTER THIS TECHNIQUE TO OVERCOME ANY FEAR
This is a time-tested procedure and an effective method for conquering anxiety that I train from my platform. Try it! You will see that it genuinely works. If you are scared of the sea, a high mountain, an interview, an audition, or even restricted spaces, this can help.

Since we were speaking of water previously, I will use it as an example. If you are afraid of swimming, you should find yourself in a solitary location and position yourself there for five to ten minutes three or four times throughout the day. Once there, just imagine that you are swimming. In reality, you are floating in your head. It is a subjective feeling. Imagine that you are projected onto the surface of the sea. You can feel the cold of the water as well as the motion of your legs and arms. It is an exhilarating, lively, and enjoyable mental activity. Keep in mind that this is not just a daydream. Instead, realize that the experience you are having will be reflected within the mind of your unconscious. In the end, you will be forced to create the exact image and similarity of the idea that you engraved on your subconscious mind in your real life. The subconscious is at work. Employ the same method to overcome your fear of high places or mountains. Imagine that you are on the mountain, experience the reality, and enjoy the view, all the while knowing that if you do this in your mind, you will soon be able to do it physically with ease.

HE BLESSED THE ELEVATOR

A friend who was an executive with a huge company was terrified to be inside an elevator. He would climb five stories for a long time to get to his office each morning. Soon, he told me that he had begun to start blessing the office's elevator in the evening and at least once throughout the day. By doing so, eventually, he was able to overcome his fears.

In performing his blessing, he spoke about the elevator several times each day, stating, "The elevator that we are using is a fantastic idea. It was born from the mind of all people. It is a blessing and opportunity for our employees. It offers excellent service. It operates in divine order. I ride through it in tranquility and happiness. I am still here now, as the flow of life, love, and understanding flow through my patterns of thinking. In my mind, I am in the elevator and step from it and into my office. The elevator is filled with our employees. I speak to them while feeling warm, joyful, happy, and completely liberated. It is an amazing feeling of freedom, faith, and trust. I thank God for it."

He continued to pray in this way for about ten days, and on the 11th day, he went into the elevator along with other group members and felt completely relaxed.

NORMAL AND ABNORMAL FEAR

Everyone on Earth is born with two fears: the fear of falling and sound. These fears act as alarms provided by nature and serve as a way to protect yourself. This normal fear is reasonable. If you hear the sound of a car speeding on the highway, you pull yourself away to avoid being hit. The fear of being crushed is dispelled through your decision. Other worries were handed to you by your parents or relatives, teachers, and everyone else who had an impact on your childhood. Many of these are abnormal fears.

ABNORMAL FEAR

The most frightening thing that can happen in connection with our fears is when people begin to let their imaginations play around. I have a friend who was invited to travel the globe via plane. In her anxiety over the situation, she began cutting out newspaper clippings containing every report of plane crashes that she saw. She repeatedly imagined herself falling into the ocean, drowning, and so on. It may seem like normal anxiety for those who fear flying—but an abnormal fear from a psychological perspective. Had she continued in this way, she could have drawn the attention of the occurrences she feared most and manifested these events into her reality.

Here is another instance of abnormal fear. I once knew a businessman living in New York who was quite prosperous. However, he had a mental motion picture for which he served as the director. He would play this mental picture, which consisted of financial failure, bankruptcy, and empty shelves over and over. In his mind, there was no balance in his bank account, and he fell into a deep depression. Since he would not put aside this depressing image, he kept telling his wife, "This cannot endure," and, "There will be a recession soon," and, "I believe we will be bankrupt." It was a self-fulfilling prophecy because of the power of his subconscious mind.

Some time later, my wife informed me that he did eventually declare bankruptcy and that all the things he had envisioned and feared were realized. The things he was afraid of did not exist; however, they were brought to life by his habit of imagining, believing, and predicting financial catastrophe. In the Bible, Job stated, "The thing I feared has happened to me."

Unfortunately, this is all too common. Many people are scared that something terrible could happen to their children or that a tragedy will happen to them. When they discover an outbreak or rare illness, people live in fear of contracting it, and others believe they are already suffering from the disease. It is an atypical worry.

THE ANSWER TO ABNORMAL FEAR

To conquer abnormal fears, you must change your mental attitude. Shift it in the opposite direction. Staying at the edge of fear means stagnation and physical and psychological decline. If fear is present, you will have the urge to do anything other than face what you fear. Focus on what you wanted rather than what you were afraid of. Immerse yourself in your passion and be aware that the subjective will always prevail over the objective. Employing this mindset will help you gain confidence and boost your spirits. The mighty potential of the subconscious is working in your direction and will not be stopped. Thus, peace and confidence are yours.

EXAMINE YOUR FEARS

A president from a major company once informed me that when he had worked as an agent, he used to stroll around the block five or six times before calling the customer. He had to muster the strength and overcome the fear of doing so. However, the sales manager came in one day and told him, "Do not be scared of the boogieman. There is not any Boogieman. It is a myth." The manager explained that every time he glanced at his fears, he confronted them head-on and looked them straight in the eyes. Then, they faded away to the point of no return.

HE LANDED IN THE JUNGLE

A chaplain shared with me his experiences during his time fighting in the Second World War. He had been forced to parachute from a damaged plane and land in the forest. He claimed he was scared. However, he was already aware that there were two types of fear: normal and abnormal. We have already discussed this.

He decided to take action to overcome the fear right away. He began to speak to himself, saying, "John, you cannot let your fear take over you. Your fear is a need for security, safety, and an escape route." Then, he would say, "Infinite intelligence, which guides the planets in their courses, is now leading and guiding me out of this jungle." He continued to repeat these words for ten minutes or longer. "Then," he added, "Something began to stir in me. A sense of confidence began to grip me, and I started to walk. After a few days, I miraculously emerged from the jungle and was brought to the helicopter that rescued me." His new mental outlook helped him to conquer his fear and recover. His trust and confidence in the wisdom and power within him solved his dilemma. He was well aware of the situation and also told me, "Had I begun to bemoan my fate and indulge my fears, I would have succumbed to the monster's fear and probably would have died of starvation."

HE DISMISSED HIMSELF

The head of an organization had said that he was worried about losing his job. For three years, he felt this way and had said it out loud on several occasions. He always imagined failing. The fear he had was not real, except as a nagging idea in his head. His vivid imagination caused a dramatization of the demise of his career, leading him to become extremely anxious. It became difficult to work under the circumstances, and he was finally asked to quit. In reality, he could not accept that he was good at his job and would hold onto it. The continual negative and fear-based thoughts in his mind led him to react and respond in such a way that caused him to make mistakes and rash choices, leading to his demise as an executive manager. The decision to dismiss him would not have occurred if he had immediately shifted his thoughts to positive and beneficial ones.

THEY PLOTTED AGAINST HIM

During a recent world lecture tour, I had a 2-hour discussion with a well-known government official. He was awestruck by the feeling of peace and tranquility he felt within himself. He claimed that all the snark he gets politically from the press and the opposition parties do not bother his peace. He credits this to a solid commitment to meditation. The way he practices is to be still for fifteen minutes each morning while realizing that within his mind exists a quiet sea of peace. Meditating gives him immense power to conquer every kind of challenge and anxiety. A while ago, an acquaintance called him late at night to inform him that a group of people was plotting against him. The way he responded was by telling his coworker, "I will go to bed tonight in peace and tranquility. You can discuss this with me later. I am available at 10:00 tomorrow morning."

He explained to me, "I believe there is no way that a negative idea or event will occur unless I emotionally believe the thought of it and accept it in my mind. I am not going to accept their notion of fear. Thus, no harm could befall me." You could sense how calm the man was. How cool, how serene! He did not get overly excited in the presence of what many would deem frightening news. There was no pulling of his hair or shaking of his hands. He had found his inner peace, the stillness of the waters, and a deep sense of tranquility.

DELIVER YOURSELF FROM ALL YOUR FEARS

Make use of this formula to get rid of anxiety. "I looked to the Lord, and He listened to my plea and delivered me from my anxieties. PSALM 34:4." The Lord is an old word that refers to law or your mind's subconscious influence. Discover the secrets of your unconscious, and learn how it operates and performs its functions. Utilize the strategies taught in this section. Apply them today—right now even! Your subconscious will react, and you will be free from all worries. "I prayed to the Lord, and He heard me and freed me from all my worries."

Identity

Positive Imagination

STEP THIS WAY FROM FEAR TO FREEDOM

Do what you are scared to do, and the end of fear is guaranteed. Say to yourself the affirmation, "I am going to master this fear," and you will. Fear is the most negative idea within your mind. Refresh your mind with a positive idea in its place, and erase the fear. Fear has claimed millions of lives, but the power of confidence is stronger than that of fear. Nothing can be more potent than faith in God and the goodness of God.

Fear is man's most formidable foe. It is the reason for illness, failure, and poor human relations. Love dispels fear. It provides us with a deep emotional connection to the beautiful things in life. Be in love with integrity, honesty, and justice, for this is a way to build a foundation for goodwill and heighten the possibility of success. Feel the euphoria present at the top and, invariably, the most awesome things will be yours.

Refuse to be scared by using something else, like "I sing beautifully; I am poised, serene, and calm." It can yield amazing results.

The fear of losing your memory is behind the type of amnesia that occurs during written and oral examinations.

You can get over this by repeatedly affirming, "I have a perfect memory for everything I need to know," or you could imagine a friend congratulating you for your outstanding performance on the exam. Be persistent, and you will be successful.

If you are scared to swim, try swimming. In your imagination, you can swim in a free and joyful manner. Imagine yourself in the water with the power of your thoughts. Feel the excitement and chill of splashing across the pool. It should be vivid. If you can do this objectively, you will feel compelled to dive deep into the water and overcome it. It is the rule of your brain.

Suppose you are afraid of enclosed or crowded places like lectures halls or elevators. You can imagine yourself in an elevator, praising every part and function of its mechanical components. You will be amazed by how quickly your fear will vanish.

The only fears you were born with are the fear of falling and sound. The rest of your fears came from your childhood. Eliminate them.

Normal fear is beneficial. Atypical fear is extremely harmful and destructive. The frequent relapse into fears can lead to abnormal obsession and even deep complexes. The constant fear of something can trigger feelings of fear and anxiety. However, you can overcome the fear of the abnormal by recognizing the power of your subconscious mind. It can alter the conditions and fulfill the desires you have in your heart. Start paying attention immediately and devote yourself to your goal, which is the exact opposite of your fears. That is what love is. It takes out fear.

If you are scared of failing, put all of your focus on success. Believe it to be so. If you are afraid of sickness, think about yourself in perfect health and wellness. If you are scared about an injury, focus on the protection and guidance of God. If you are afraid of dying, focus on Eternal Life. God is Life, and that is your present life.

The supreme law of substitution provides the answer to anxiety. Anything you are afraid of has a solution within your desires. If you are sick, you desire health. Suppose you are fear being a prisoner and want to be free. Think of freedom! Be prepared for the positive. Concentrate on the good and beneficial, and be aware that your subconscious mind will answer you every single time. It will never fail.

The things you are afraid of are not real; they exist only as thoughts within your head. Thoughts are a source of creativity. This is why Job declared, "The thing I was afraid of is now upon me," in the Bible.

Examine your fears and see them in the light of logic. Learn to smile in the face of your worries, for it is the most effective treatment.

There is nothing that can disturb you more than your own thinking. The comments, suggestions, or threats made by others are not threats to your wellbeing. That power lies only within you. If your focus is on the good and positive, God's power is in your positive thoughts. The only true thing about God is His creative power, which is harmonious. There is no division or disagreement within it. Its root is only in love. It is the reason God's power is shown through your thoughts of goodness.

HOW YOUR SUBCONSCIOUS REMOVES MENTAL BLOCKS

The answer lies in the issue itself. The answer lies in every question. If you find yourself facing a problem and cannot see which path to take, it is best to believe that the infinite mind within the subconscious mind knows everything and is sharing all of the answers with you right now. Your new perspective brought to you through your subconscious intelligence will bring about an amicable solution that you will soon discover. You can be assured that this mindset will bring peace, order, and meaning to all of your activities.

HOW TO BREAK OR BUILD A HABIT

You are a product of habit. Habits are the functions that your mind's subconscious performs. You learned how to swim, cycle, dance, and drive a car by consciously doing these activities repeatedly until they carved out a path within your mind's subconscious. In the end, the autopilot behavior associated with your subconscious assumed control. This is often referred to as something becoming second nature. It is a reaction your unconscious mind has to how you think and what you do.

You are free to pick habits that are good or bad, beneficial or harmful. If you continue to repeat the same negative thoughts or actions for an extended period, you will be subject to the pressure of those thoughts becoming habitual. The rule of your subconscious is compulsive.

HOW HE BROKE A BAD HABIT

Mr. Jones said to me, "An uncontrollable urge to drink overwhelms me, and I am drunk for up to two weeks at a time. I cannot quit this horrible habit!" Many times, this happened to the man. He was a victim of the routine of drinking in excess. Even though he started drinking out of his own volition, somewhere along that way, he began to recognize that he could change his habits and create new ones. However, he stated that although he had first felt determination and realized it was possible to control his cravings for a short time, his ongoing efforts to ward off the numerous cravings for alcohol only led to more problems. His repeated failures convinced him that he was a hopeless case and was simply unable to control the urge or desire. Unfortunately, the idea that he was powerless served as a powerful nudge in his mind, increasing his vulnerability and making his life into a string of mistakes and poor choices.

Fortunately, I taught him how to integrate the work of the subconscious and conscious mind. I explained that when they cooperate and work together, the thought or desire stored in the subconscious mind can be realized. The mind of reason recognized that if the previous routine or track led him to trouble, it was possible to create an alternative path to peace, sobriety, calmness, and clarity of thought. He recognized that his destructive habits had become controlled by auto-pilot, but it resulted from his conscious decision. He realized that even if he was negatively conditioned, he could be positively conditioned to make a positive change. In the end, he stopped thinking about the notion that he was in no position to break his drinking habit. Furthermore, he realized that there was no barrier to his healing that was not stemming from his own thoughts.

THE POWER OF HIS MENTAL PICTURE

The man developed a habit of putting his body into a relaxed state and then becoming drowsy and calm. He then flooded his mind with images of his desired outcome with the knowledge that his subconscious would bring it to fruition in the most effective method. He imagined his daughter being happy for his freedom and telling him, "Daddy, it is wonderful to be at home!" He had already lost his family members due to his use of alcohol. He was not permitted to visit them, and his wife refused to communicate with him.

During his regular schedule, he was able to sit down and contemplate how the mental picture that illustrated his contentedness was laid out. When his attention had diverted the mind, he established an automatic habit to remember the mental image of his daughter's smile and the scene in the house that was enlivened by her cheerful voice. It led to an improvement in his mental state. It was an incremental process, but he continued it. He was determined to keep going, believing that, eventually, he would create an entirely new pattern of behavior in his subconscious mind.

I explained to my client that I thought of his mind's consciousness like a camera, and that the unconscious mind served as the plate that he used to register and engrave the image. This seemed to make a lasting impression on him, and his main goal became to imprint the image on his mind and then develop it.

Films are made in darkness; similarly, mental images are created within the mind's darkroom.

The Drama Trainagle

Forgive the past

My-mindguide.com

FOCUSED ATTENTION

Contemplating that his mind was merely the camera, he put in little mental effort. He knew it was not a mental fight. Instead, he slowed down his thinking and kept his focus on that single scene until he became more familiar with it. He was absorbed by the mental stage, repeating the mental movie often in his mind. There was no doubt that recovery would occur. If there were a temptation for drinking, the man would shift his mind from any imaginings of drunkenness to the warm and welcoming sensation of being home with his family. He finally succeeded due to his confidence in seeing the image forming within his mind. He is now the president of a multimillion-dollar company and is extremely happy.

HE SAID A JINX WAS FOLLOWING HIM

Mr. Bloch, a salesman, said that he had been making a monthly income of $ 7000,00, but that for the last three months, the doors seemed to be blocked to any progress. He had clients come to the point of putting their signatures on the dotted line, but at the eleventh hour, the door shut. He suggested that perhaps there was a jinx following him. I soon discovered that, three months prior, Mr. Bloch had been distraught, angry, and bitter at a dentist who, after having promised that he would sign an agreement, was unable to sign at the end of the day. He started to live with a fear in his unconscious that others might do the same, creating a pattern of hostility, frustration, and hurdles. He slowly cultivated in his mind an idea of constant obstructions and last-minute cancellations until a vicious circle was created. "The terrifying thing that I have ever experienced is what has happened to me," Mr. Bloch informed me, realizing that the issue was with his mind and that it was vital to change his mindset if he was to succeed.

His string of misfortunes ended when he employed the following method. He would state, "I realize I am one with the incomparable power in my mind, and that I can overcome any obstacle, challenge or delay. I am living in the joyful expectation of the greatest things to come. My subconscious mind responds in response to the thoughts I have. I am aware that the inexhaustible power of my subconscious can never be stopped. Infinite intelligence will always succeed at whatever task it is beginning. The creative mind works in me, bringing my ideas and goals to fruition. What I do, I will carry to a satisfying conclusion. My goal with my work is to offer an excellent service. All people I meet are thankful for the services I provide. Everything I do comes to fruition in perfect order."

This prayer was repeated every morning just before calling on his clients. It was also his habit to pray each night before going to bed. This was established as a new pattern of behavior within his subconscious mind in just a short period, and he was back to his usual pace as a successful salesperson.

HOW MUCH DO YOU WANT WHAT YOU WANT?

A young man once asked the philosopher Socrates how he could gain wisdom. Socrates responded, "Come with me." He took the young man to the river and dragged the boy's head beneath the water, holding it under until the boy gasped for air. Only then did Socrates relax his grip and let his head rise to the surface. Once the boy regained his breath, Socrates asked him, "What did you desire most when you were underwater?"

"I wanted air," said the boy.

Socrates responded, "When you want wisdom as much as you wanted air while you were immersed in the water, you will receive it."

When you genuinely are driven to overcome any obstacle within your own life, then make a clear conclusion that there is an escape route, and that is the path you want to take, then success and happiness are guaranteed. If you desire calm and peace, you can attain it. However you have been treated, however unfair your boss was, or however sly a criminal someone you trusted has proven to be, it becomes irrelevant to you once you are awake to your spiritual and mental capabilities. At that point, you already know what you want, and you will adamantly resist allowing thoughts of hate, hostility, anger, or illness to take away your peace, well-being, harmony, and joy. By aligning your thoughts and directing them toward your life goals, you will stop being irritated by circumstances, people, news, events, or conditions. The goal is health, peace, harmony, inspiration, and prosperity. You will see a stream of tranquility flowing within your body. Your thoughts are the intangible and unimaginable power. You can let it be blessed, inspire, and provide you with peace.

WHY HE COULD NOT BE HEALED

Let's take a moment to look at a detailed case study of a man who was married with four children, sustaining an external relationship, and living in secret with a woman during his business travels. He was anxious, sick, irritable, cantankerous, and could not sleep without medication—and even then had difficulty. The medication prescribed by his doctor could not reduce his blood pressure, which had reached higher than 200. He experienced constant pains throughout the organs in his body, which doctors could neither identify nor alleviate. To add insult to his many injuries, he was also drinking frequently.

The root of these many issues was a profound feeling of guilt. He had sinned against his marriage vows, which irked him. The religion that he was taught was deeply embedded in his mind's subconscious, and he was drinking heavily to heal the wounds of guilt. Some people suffering from an illness will take morphine or codeine to ease their physical pain, whereas this man was drinking alcohol to heal the pain within his mind. The alcohol merely added fuel to the flames.

THE EXPLANATION AND THE CURE

This man was enthralled by explanations of how the brain functioned. He was confronted by his problems, then reflected on them, and resigned from his job, which required a great deal of travel. He realized that his drinking reflected a subconscious desire to flee. Once the hidden reason for his reliance on alcohol within his subconscious was eliminated, then healing would ensue.

The man began impressing his mind's subconscious at least three times a day with this prayer: "My brain is filled with calm, poise, and balance. The infinite is a blissful peace within me. It recalls anything that has happened in the past, future, or even the present. The infinity within my mind guides me in every way. I can now face any situation confidently, with poise, tranquility, and confidence. I am now free of my old habits. My mind is filled with peace, joy, and happiness. I accept my forgiveness, and my forgiveness is granted. Sobriety, peace, and faith are the utmost in my thoughts."

The prayer was repeated frequently, consciously, with purpose, and with a deep awareness of his actions and the reason behind them. Knowing the purpose behind his actions provided him with faith. He was taught that when he spoke these phrases slowly, steadily, and with love and meaning, the words would slowly recede into his subconscious mind. As seeds, they will expand after their species. These truths, which he focused on, came through his eyes. His ears heard it, and the healing vibrations from these words flooded the subconscious mind and destroyed any negative mental patterns that had caused the problems. Light dispels darkness. Positive thought dispels negative. He was transformed within a matter of a month.

REFUSING TO ADMIT IT

If you are an alcohol or drug user, acknowledge that you are. Do not hide the fact. Many people continue to drink because they do not want to admit it to themselves or the world.

Your problem is insecurity and inner anxiety. You refuse to face the world, so you attempt to escape your obligations by drinking. If you are an alcoholic, you are not free to choose even though you believe you are. You might even boast about your willpower. If you are a frequent drinking addict and declare, "I will not touch it anymore," you will be unable to bring this statement to reality since you do not know where to find the strength. You live in the mental prison you created, governed by your convictions, opinions, training, and influences. Like many people are, you are a creature of habit. You are trained to respond to the way you react.

BUILDING IN THE IDEA OF FREEDOM

You can infuse the concept of peace and a tranquil mind deep into your mind until it can penetrate the depths of your subconscious. This will remove any desire for alcohol from your mind as an all-powerful force. You will then be able to understand how your brain works, and you will be able to prove your claim and prove it to yourself. You can and will stop relying on alcohol.

FIFTY-ONE PERCENT HEALED

If you have a burning determination to get rid of any harmful habit, you are already fifty-one percent healed. If you are more motivated by a desire to let go of the destructive habit rather than keep it going, you will not have any difficulty attaining absolute freedom from it. Whatever idea you anchor your mind on, the second will magnify. If you focus your mind on the notion of liberation—freedom from routine—or peace of mind, you direct your attention on this area; you create emotions and feelings that eventually emotionalize the idea of peace and freedom. Any suggestion that you emotionally connect to is accepted by your subconscious mind and is realized.

THE LAW OF SUBSTITUTION

Consider the possibility that something good will be derived from your pain. Your suffering is not for nothing. It is, however, stupid to endure suffering. If you remain an alcohol user, it can result in physical and mental decline and degeneration. Be aware that the power of your mind is helping you. Although you might feel a bit depressed, try to envision the happiness of freedom waiting for you. It is the rule of a substitute. Your imagination led you to the bottle. Let it lead you to peace and a tranquil mind. You may suffer some in the process, but it serves a goal. You will be able to bear it as motherhood in the throes of childbirth. Moreover, you will also birth a child from the mind. Your subconscious will be the first to give birth to sobriety.

CAUSE OF ALCOHOLISM

The root of the alcoholism problem is destructive and harmful thinking. Alcoholics have a profound sense of inadequacy, feel defeated, and often fall prey to anger, accompanied by intense inner hostility. There are many excuses for drinking; however, the main motive lies in the drinker's mental life.

THREE MAGIC STEPS

The first step is to still and quiet the wheels of your mind. Enter into a sleepy, drowsy state. In this calm, relaxed, open state, you prepare for the next step. Think of a short phrase that can easily be engraved in the memory and play it repeatedly in your mind to create music. Make use of the words: "Sobriety and peace of mind are mines now, and for that, I give thanks." To stop your mind from wandering, sing the phrase aloud or draw its pronunciation with your tongue and lips while you sing it out loud. This will help it enter your subconscious. Try this for five minutes or more. You will experience a profound emotional reaction.

Third, before getting ready to go to sleep, try the things Johann von Goethe, a German author, did. Imagine a friend or someone you love before you. The eyes are closed, and you are relaxed and content. The person you love or adore is in the present moment and tells you, "Congratulations!" You can see their smile and hear the sound of their voice in your mind. You think about touching their hand. It is the real thing, and the experience is vibrant. The word "congratulations" implies complete liberty. Repeat this until you have the unconscious reaction that will satisfy.

KEEP ON KEEPING ON

When you feel fear knocking on the doors of your thoughts or notice anxiety occupying your mind, stop and note your dream, your objective. Consider the unlimited power of your subconscious mind. This power can be generated by your imagination and thinking to give you confidence, strength, and courage. Be persistent, and keep going until the day ends and the shadows fade away.

REVIEW YOUR THOUGHT POWER

Within every question lies an answer. Infinite intelligence will respond to you whenever you invoke it with confidence and faith. Habits are formed by the work that your mind's subconscious does. There is no better proof of the incredible potential of your unconscious than the influence it exerts on your daily life. You are a product of habit. Habit patterns are formed in your subconscious mind by repeating the same thought or action until it is a part of the mind's subconscious and becomes automatic, such as dancing, swimming, walking, typing, or driving your car.

You can are responsible for making your own choices. You can pick healthy habits or harmful ones. Praying is a good habit. Any mental image, supported by faith, is what you view in your subconscious mind while your unconscious mind brings it to fruition. The biggest obstacle to your success and accomplishing your goals is your thoughts or image. If your mind strays elsewhere, return it to your purpose or ideal. Do this regularly. It is known as disciplining the mind. Your mind's consciousness is your camera, and your unconscious mind is the sensor where you record or imprint the image.

The only thing that can follow any person is a fear-based thought repeated throughout the brain. Stop the jinx by recognizing that whatever you begin, you will come to an end in perfect order. Visualize your happy ending, and hold it in your mind with the confidence that you will see it through.

To establish an entirely new habit, you must first convince yourself that it is beneficial. If your desire to end the harmful practice is higher than your desire to maintain it, you are already fifty-one percent healed.

Other people's words cannot harm you unless they have a basis in your mental involvement. Set your sights on your goals: harmony, peace, and happiness.

Drinking is a manifestation of a subconscious wish to flee. The reason for alcoholism is destructive and harmful thinking.

The remedy is to imagine freedom, sobriety, and perfection, and you will then experience the satisfaction of success. Many people continue to drink because they do not want to admit their reliance on alcohol. Once you accept that you have a problem, the laws in your unconscious mind that bind you and impede your freedom to move will allow you to be free and happy. It is contingent on the way you apply it.

Your imagination led you to the end of the road, causing the problem. Now, let it lead you to freedom—by believing you are free. The root of alcoholism is destructive and harmful thinking; thus, the solution is shifting to positive thinking and forming new habits in the subconscious mind. Let your heart lead your thoughts, which will influence your behavior.

If fear is knocking at the entrance of your thoughts, put your confidence in God and everything positive to unlock the door to happiness.

Let Go Process

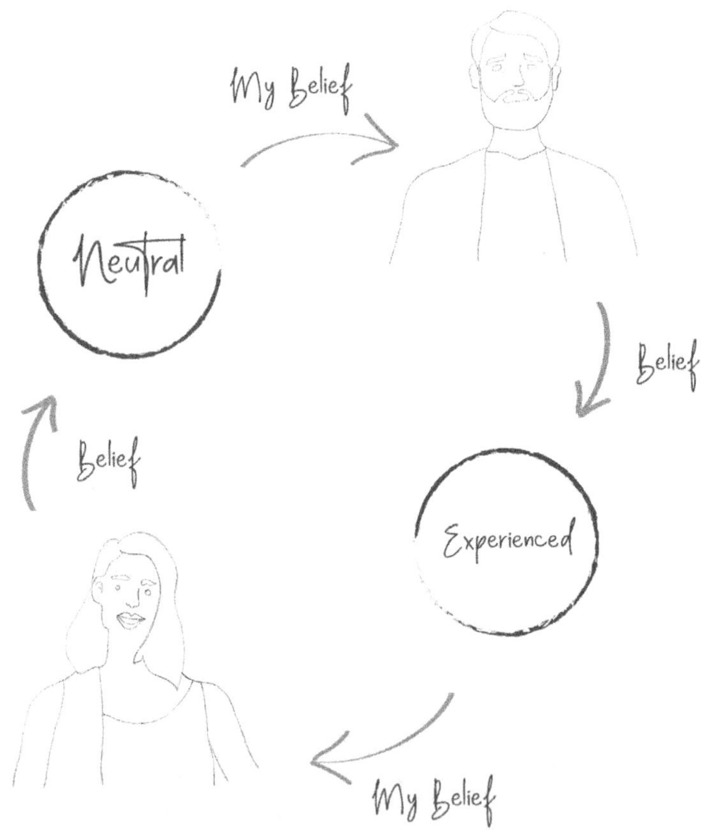

MARITAL PROBLEMS AND THE SUBCONSCIOUS MIND

Inadequate understanding of the powers and functions of the brain is the source of marital conflict in all its forms. Properly using the laws of the mind will resolve the conflict between spouses, effectively healing the relationship. Through prayer, couples can remain together despite their past challenges. The contemplation of God's ideals paired with the study of life principles, agreement on a shared purpose and plan, and the satisfaction of freedom of choice will result in a harmonious union. Through the power of the subconscious, you can unlock the great bliss of wedlock and a powerful feeling of unity in which the two have become one.

So, when is the best time to work toward a successful marriage? The ideal time to avoid divorce is before the wedding. While it is not a bad idea to seek escape from a challenging situation, it is essential to consider the issues that caused the problems initially. Isn't it better to pay attention to the root of marital conflict? In other words, to get right to the heart of the situation in question?

Typically, annulment, divorce, separation, and the resulting endless legal battles are directly linked to insufficient knowledge of the interrelationship and the functioning of the subconscious and conscious mind.

THE MEANING OF MARRIAGE

For marriage to be authentic, it must be based on a spiritual foundation. It should come from the heart, which is the cup of love. Honesty, sincerity, and kindness are each a different kind of love. Every couple should be honest and genuine to each other. It is not a real wedding when one weds another individual to increase wealth status in society or build one's self-esteem. These reasons show a lack of sincerity, honesty, integrity, and genuine love. A marriage like this is a fake—nothing more than a sham. If a woman claims, "I am tired working; I want to get married because I want security," her reasoning is not based upon true love. She is not correctly utilizing the law of mind. Her security is only contingent upon her understanding of the interplay between the subconscious and conscious mind and its application.

A woman, for instance, will never be in desperate need of money or health if she follows the strategies described in the chapters of this book. She will earn her wealth without the assistance of her father, husband, or anyone else, if that is her desire. The woman should not be dependent on her husband for happiness, health, peace, motivation, guidance, love, prosperity, security, joy, or anything else in this world. Instead, a sense of confidence and tranquility will result from knowing the inner forces and using the law of mind to make decisions positively.

HOW TO ATTRACT THE IDEAL HUSBAND

You have now mastered how your mind's subconscious works. You know that whatever you think about will be reflected in your world. Start now to impress upon your mind a display of the traits and qualities you most desire in a man.

The following is a fantastic method for achieving your ideal spouse: Sit down in your recliner or another peaceful, comfortable space at night. Close your eyes, release any tension, and relax your body, allowing yourself to become very calm, passive, and receptive. Engage your subconscious mind and tell it, "I am currently attracting a man to my life who is sincere, honest, and loyal. He is faithful and happy. He is peaceful, serene, and successful. These traits I admire are settling into my subconscious mind right now. These traits become part of me, embedded in my subconscious when I think about them. I am aware of an irresistible law of attraction and that I draw to myself the person I want to attract according to my own subconscious beliefs. I receive what I believe to be real in my mind's subconscious."

Continue by telling yourself, "I believe I can be a part of his tranquility and joy. My ideals are dear to him, and I love his ideals. He does not want to be my savior; neither do I wish to get him to love me except for the sake of love itself. There is love between us—freedom, respect, and love."

Try this method of influencing your mind's subconscious. In the end, you will experience the great pleasure of attracting to yourself a man who has the characteristics and traits that you most desired and included in your thoughts and prayer. Your subconscious can open a path that will lead the two of you to meet based on the irresistible, ever-changing flow of your subconscious mind. You must have a strong desire to share the very best of yourself and all that you have within your heart, including love, devotion, and cooperation. Be open to the presence of love, which you have offered to the mind of your unconscious.

HOW TO ATTRACT THE IDEAL WIFE

Similarly to using the subconscious mind to bring the ideal husband, the same can be done to call the perfect wife. Find a comfortable, quiet space and get into the abovementioned conditions. Then, invoke the following: "I now attract the right woman, she who is completely in sync with me. It is a spiritual bond since the divine love operates through the persona of someone I can blend with perfectly. I am confident that I can bring peace, light, and happiness to the woman I love. I believe that I can make this woman's life complete, happy, and beautiful."

Continue to speak, stating, "I now declare that she is blessed with the following attributes and qualities that make her spiritually reliable, loyal, and trustworthy. She is serene, tranquil, and content. We are irresistibly attracted to one another. Only what is part of love, beauty, truth, and honesty will come into my world. I have accepted my ideal friend right now."

If you take a moment to think calmly and with interest about the characteristics and traits you will most appreciate in the person you want to meet, you will create the equivalent mental image within your mind. Then, your subconscious's more powerful mental tidal waves will bring you into divine harmony, and you will meet and experience a special connection with your spouse.

NO NEED FOR A THIRD MISTAKE

A teacher recently told me, "I have been married to three different men, and all of them have been submissive, passive, and dependent upon me when it comes to making final decisions and controlling everything. Why am I attracted to such men?"

I asked her if she knew that her second husband was this type of man, and she responded, "Of course not. If I had known, I might not have gotten married to him." It appears that she did not learn a valuable lesson from her first error. The issue was, in fact, her appearance. She was very masculine and domineering and unconsciously desired her man to be at ease and passive so that she could play the role of the dominant one. It was all an unconscious motive, and her subconscious image attracted what she believed to be desirable. She was required to break free from the habit by adopting the correct prayer method.

BREAKING THE NEGATIVE PATTERN

The woman realized a fundamental fact. If you believe you will be with the kind of man you imagine, it will be done to you. The following are the particular prayers she used to overcome the old pattern of her subconscious and draw to her the perfect partner: "I am building into my mind the kind of man I want. I want to attract the man as my husband is powerful, strong, loving, extremely masculine, honest, successful, loyal, faithful, and trustworthy. He has found love and joy with me. I love following wherever the Lord is leading."

"I am aware that he is looking for me, and I am willing to share myself with him. I am sincere, honest, loving, kind, and caring. I have many wonderful attributes to give to him, including goodwill, a happy heart, and a well-balanced body. He is willing to give me the identical in return. It is mutual. I give and receive. The divine intelligence knows where this man is, and the greater understanding of my subconscious is now bringing us together uniquely and in the best possible way. We will instantly recognize each other. I give this wish to my mind's subconscious, who knows how to bring my dream to reality. I am grateful for the perfect solution, which I know I will receive."

She prayed in this manner both morning and night to affirm these truths, aware that she could attain the mental state to lead her to what she was looking for through the constant use of the mind.

THE ANSWER TO HER PRAYER

A few months passed. During that time, the woman attended many social engagements and went on several dates that were not acceptable to her. As she began to ask questions or doubt her thoughts and inclinations, she reaffirmed her prayers and knew that her infinite wisdom would bring it all to fruition according to its plan—and that there was nothing about to worry. The final decree of her divorce proceedings was approved, and she immediately felt relief and mental peace come over her.

Soon after, she went to work as a receptionist at a doctor's office. She shared with me that she knew that the doctor was the one as soon as she met him. He was aware of it as well, as he had proposed to her on the very first day she entered the office! Their marriage was blissfully happy. The doctor was neither passive nor submissive, a former football player and an exceptional athlete. In addition, he was a profoundly religious man, even though he was free of any organized religion or specific religious affiliation.

The woman in this story received precisely what she wanted because she believed in it in her mind right through to the threshold of completeness. She experienced the complete emotional and mental joining of her thoughts, which became part of her.

SHOULD I GET A DIVORCE?

Divorce is a unique and very individual issue. In some instances, there was no need for marriage in the first place. Divorce could be the right choice for one individual and unjust for another. For example, a divorced woman might be more honest and noble than her married sisters, living a life of deceit.

I once spoke to a woman whose spouse was an alcoholic, ex-convict, abuser of wives, and a non-provider. The woman, however, was told that it was not right to get divorced. Hearing this, I said to her that marriage should be a product of the heart. That is, the perfect marriage involves two seats that can blend harmoniously with love and sincerity. The sole action of compassion is to love.

She decided she knew what she needed to do based on this explanation. She became aware that no law of God required her to be brow-beaten and intimidated because she had been told, "I now pronounce you man and wife." She knew she deserved better—she earned a valid marriage brought from the shared love of two people.

If you ever doubt what to do, you can ask for help. There is always an answer within your mind, and you will receive it. Follow the guidance that comes to you through the silence of your mind. It will speak to you with tranquility.

DRIFTING INTO DIVORCE

A young couple had been married for just about a month, and already they sought a divorce. I learned that the young man of the couple lived with the constant worry that his wife might abandon him. He was deeply frightened of rejection, which had convinced him that she was being unfaithful. These thoughts haunted him and became a recurring addiction. His attitude towards life was one of suspicion and separation. He was unresponsive to her in countless ways, and his sense of separation and loss ran through their relationship.

It led to the conflict until it finally created the act that was in tune with the underlying mental model. There is always an act and reaction, also known as cause and consequence. The reaction response to our subconscious minds is called the response. In the end, his wife left the house and demanded a divorce, which is what he was worried about and believed that she would do.

DIVORCE BEGINS WITHIN THE MIND

Divorce is first conceived in mind; then, the legal process is followed. The two young people above were awash with resentment comprised of fear, doubt, and anger. These attitudes can weaken, exhaust, and make the whole body weak. The couple soon discovered that hatred divides and love brings people together.

Fortunately, they realized what they were doing with the power of their minds. As they had previously been unaware of regulating their mental actions, they wasted their minds, causing chaos and despair in their relationship. However, after my advice and a great deal of prayer therapy, the two of them came back together. They began radiating peace, love, and goodwill to one another, as every couple should. They partnered during the reading of Psalms each evening. Their relationship is becoming more beautiful with each passing day.

THE NAGGING WIFE

The most common reason a wife is irritable is that she does not feel she receives enough interest or attention from her spouse. It is usually a simple matter of the desire for affection and love. Make sure to pay attention to your wife and express your gratitude for the things she does. Honor and praise her good qualities. The most annoying woman is determined to force the man to adhere to her particular style. This is probably the most efficient method to eliminate a man from a woman's life. To maintain a happy and successful relationship, both husband and wife must stop scavenging to find tiny mistakes or faults. Instead, each should pay attention to and praise the good in one another and see the positive qualities.

THE BROODING HUSBAND

If a husband becomes angry at his wife based on things she has said or done and expresses this through the thoughts in his mind, he is engaging in adultery in a psychological sense. One of the essential meanings in the affair is idolatry, i.e., paying attention or relating with harmful and destructive responses. If a person is unconsciously resentful of his wife and full of internal hatred or disdain, he is not faithful. He is not being loyal or trustworthy to the vows he made to his wife, which state that he would love and cherish her throughout his existence.

An angry, bitter, and resentful person can often conceal these sharp thoughts and words or stifle their anger for a long time. He may take great pains to be externally courteous and friendly. He can slyly avoid anyone knowing of his underlying thoughts. Fortunately, by praising and focusing on his mental efforts, it is possible to break out of the cycle of apathy and become a better spouse. If he successfully commits to this goal, in the end, he will be able to communicate better—and not just in his relationship with his wife but also with colleagues and clients in his career. Imagine a harmonious environment, and you will eventually find peace.

THE GREAT MISTAKE

Let it be known here and now that it is an enormous mistake to discuss marital issues or conflicts with your neighbors, friends, and family members. Let us say, for instance; an unhappy wife tells her neighbor, "John does not even give me money. He treats my mother terribly, drinks far too much, and is verbally abusive and insulting." This is an extreme error in judgment.

If the wife has been making fun of her husband and shaming him before others, he is no longer the ideal husband to these people. Do not discuss your marital troubles with anyone else unless you are under the guidance of a trained counselor. Others will be negative about your marriage, which you may not want should you make amends. In addition, when you discuss and dwell on your spouse's flaws, you are creating these thoughts in your mind. At this point in the book, you know what the results of that will be.

Family members cannot be counted on, as they are biased and may, therefore, provide you with the wrong advice, regardless of what they believe is best for you. Any suggestion that violates the golden rule, a universal law, is not good or solid. It is important to remember that no two humans ever lived under the same roof without some level of conflict of personalities and moments of stress or pain. Do not show this negative side of your relationship to acquaintances. Instead, keep your disagreements to yourselves. And always beware of criticism or the condemnation of your spouse.

DO NOT TRY TO ALTER YOUR WIFE FOR YOUR PURPOSES

A husband should not attempt to change or alter his wife to a new version to suit his whims or ideas of how she should look or act. A tactless effort to alter her in various ways is not a decision that she has actively come to on her own and is, therefore, a naïve attempt at improving her for your selfish purposes. The results frequently lead to the breakup of the marriage. The attempts to change her character will likely destroy her self-confidence and pride while creating a sense of hostility and resentment, which can be fatal to the marriage bond.

Changes are required on occasion, obviously, for our health and wellbeing, but if you take an in-depth look at yourself or your spouse, you will find many flaws as you study behavior and character. No one is perfect in the eyes of everyone else.

These flaws, once discovered, will be a constant distraction for the remainder of your marriage. Do not go looking for things to change! If you go into a marriage thinking, "I will make him over into what I want," you are looking for trouble and likely headed to divorce court. You are asking for suffering and will probably have to discover the hard way that no one else but oneself can make real change.

PRAY TOGETHER AND STAY TOGETHER

The first rule is never to carry the accumulated anger that comes from minor disappointments from day-to-day. Make sure you forgive each other for any lack of vigor before you go to bed in the evening. As you get up at dawn, you should claim that infinite wisdom guides you through all of your choices. Send your positive thoughts of harmony, peace, and love to your spouse—as well as to everyone else within your family and across the entire world.

The next step is to say grace during breakfast. Thank God for the delicious food you eat, for the abundance of it, and for all of your blessings. Ensure that no worries or disagreements are brought up in the early morning conversations; this is also true during dinnertime. Speak to your spouse or partner, telling them, "I appreciate all you are doing, and I radiate love and goodwill to you all day long."

The third step is that the spouse and husband should alternate during the nighttime prayers. Do not take your spouse for granted. Show them a bounty of appreciation and love. Focus on acts of gratitude and goodwill instead of resentment or nagging. The best way to enjoy a peaceful and happy environment in your marriage is to build the base from beauty, love, harmony, mutual respect, faith in God, and everything else that is good. Take a look at the 23rd, 27th, and 91st Psalms, Chapter 11 of Hebrews, I Corinthians 13th Chapter, and other texts from the Bible every night before bed. If you follow these principles, your marriage will be more blessed every day throughout the years.

REVIEW YOUR ACTIONS

Inadequate understanding of spiritual and mental laws is the cause of every marital problem. However, scientifically, you are much more likely to remain in your relationship when you pray together.

The ideal time to avoid divorce is before even speaking your marriage vows. If you can learn to pray correctly, you will find the perfect partner.

A valid marriage is the union of a couple joined through the love of their lives. Their hearts beat in unison, and they go onward upwards and to God.

The marriage vows are not meant to bring happiness. Instead, happiness is found by dwelling on God's eternal truths and the transcendental tenets of living a positive life filled with good thoughts. This way, both the man and woman can be a part of one other's happiness.

You can attract the perfect partner by thinking about the traits and qualities you most appreciate in a lady or man. Then, your subconscious mind will join you with the best possible spouse in perfect order.

You must build into your thoughts the mental image of what you desire in a partner. If you are looking to attract an honest and sincere companion to your life, it is essential to be frank, passionate, open and devoted to yourself.

There is no need to make the same mistakes again and again in life or marriage. If you genuinely believe that you will have the woman or man you imagine, the world will show you the way.

To believe means to accept that something is true. Think of your ideal companion now in your mind. Do not worry about whether, when, or where you will meet the person. Rely on to the wisdom that is in your mind. It is equipped with an innate "know-how," and you do not need to support it.

You are mentally divorced if you engage in thoughts of anger, grudges, ill will, or hostility towards your spouse. Your mind is dwelling on errors rather than positive attributes. Make sure you keep your vows to marriage, including: "I promise to cherish, love, and honor him (or her) all the days of my life."

Stop imposing fear-based patterns on your partner in marriage. Spread love, harmony, peace, and goodwill, and your wedding will become better and more beautiful over time.

Send love, peace, and goodwill to one another. Your subconscious mind will pick upbuild these positive vibrations and establish mutual trust, love, and respect.

A wife constantly seeking attention and recognition searches for affection and love. Honor and praise her for her many positive skills and attributes.

A man in love with his wife will never commit any unkind or unloving act in a manner, words, or behavior. The definition of love is simply that it is the act of loving.

When you have marital troubles, always seek advice from a professional as to go elsewhere with these issues would be like visiting a carpenter to fix a tooth. In particular, you should not discuss your marital problems with your family, friends, or neighbors. You should consult an expert for advice.

Do not try to change your husband or wife to feel better about yourself. It is always a mistake and can ruin self-confidence and pride. In addition, it creates anger that could be fatal to the marital bond. Stop trying to make the second version of yourself.

Prayer together, and you will remain together. Prayers that are scientifically based can solve all problems. Visualize your wife as she should be—healthy, joyful, happy, and beautiful. Consider your husband as he should be—strong, loved, gentle, and peaceful. Keep this image in your mind, and you will be able to experience the perfect marriage by heaven that is filled with harmony and peace.

YOUR SUBCONSCIOUS MIND AND YOUR HAPPINESS

William James, the father of American psychology, believed that the most significant discovery of the 19th century did not lie within the realm of physical science. The most important breakthrough was in the ability of our subconscious, which was triggered by faith. Within every human being is the power of infinity, which can overcome any challenge in this world.

Beautiful and lasting happiness can be found in your life when you realize that you can conquer any weakness. That will be the day you finally recognize that your subconscious can help you overcome your challenges, restore your body, and boost your success and happiness beyond the limits of your greatest dreams.

You may have experienced a profound feeling of happiness when your child was born, on the day that you were married, upon completing your college degree, or even when you were awarded a distinct honor. You may have been delighted when you were engaged to a gorgeous woman or the most attractive man. You can count the many times that have brought you happiness. However, regardless of how incredible these experiences may be, they do not provide lasting satisfaction. They are only temporary. The Book of Proverbs answers: whomever beliefs in the Lord is blessed. When you trust God the Lord (the ability and intelligence that your mind has) to guide, lead to, direct, and govern every step of your way, you will find yourself calm and at peace. If you radiate love, peace, and peace of mind to everyone around you, you are truly building a foundation of happiness for all of the days of your existence.

YOU MUST CHOOSE HAPPINESS

Happiness is an attitude of mind. The Bible states, "Pick a day whom you will serve. You are free to choose your happiness." It may sound like a simple concept, and it is pretty simple. This is perhaps why many people fail to see the path to pure happiness. They do not realize the simple nature of this path. The best things in life are easy, lively, and imaginative. They bring with them happiness and well-being. St. Paul reveals to you exactly how to imagine this life of vitality and joy in these words: "Lastly, brothers, whatever things are truthful, whatever things are honest, whatever things are fair, whatever things are pure, all things are wonderful, and all things are in good taste and if they have any virtue and there is any praise, consider these things." PHIL. 4:8.

HOW TO CHOOSE HAPPINESS

You can choose happiness at any time. Make the decision now to be happy. Here is how you accomplish it: As you wake up in the morning, repeat to yourself, "Divine order will take the reigns of my day today. Everything is working together to benefit me today. It is a brand new and amazing moment for me. There will not be another day quite like this. God guides me throughout the day, and everything I do will be successful. God's love surrounds me and envelopes me. I can go forward in tranquility. If my attention drifts away from good and constructive things, I will instantly return to its focus on only beautiful and good quality things. I am a mental and spiritual magnet, attracting all things that favor and bless me. I will succeed in my endeavors today. I am sure to be content throughout the day."

Every day should begin with this approach. By doing so, you are actively choosing happiness daily and will undoubtedly become a radiantly joyful person.

HE MADE IT A HABIT TO BE HAPPY

A few years ago, I stayed for a few days in a farmer's house in Connemara on the western coast of Ireland. He was always singing and whistling and was hilarious with jokes and good humor. I asked him to reveal the source of his happiness, and he replied, "It is a habit for me to be happy. Every day when I wake up, and at night before going to bed, I pray for my family, my animals, the crops, and I praise God for the bounty of the harvest." The farmer held a habit of happiness for nearly forty years. You know that thoughts that are repeated frequently and regularly are absorbed into the subconscious's mind and eventually become routine. He found that a beautiful life full of joy can form good habits.

YOU MUST DESIRE TO BE HAPPY

There is a crucial aspect of being satisfied with your life. It is essential to want to be content truly and deeply within yourself. Many people have been unhappy, depressed, and sad until they were suddenly uplifted by some fantastic, happy, and excellent news. excellent this state of joy, they become like a woman who told me, "It is wrong to be so happy!" They have become so used to the old mental habits that they are not happy at home in their joy! Instead, they want to return to their previous depressed and unhappy state out of a yearning for the comfort they get from what they know.

I learned about a lady in England who suffered from rheumatism for several years. She would take a pat across the knee and then say, "My rheumatism is bad today. I am not able to leave the house. My rheumatism keeps me miserable." The elderly lady was the subject of lots of attention from her children, grandchildren, and neighbors. She was determined to be acknowledged for her rheumatism and refused perfectly acceptable treatments. She was happy with the "misery," as she called it. In truth, this woman did not wish to be satisfied. The physician suggested treatment to her. A Therapist wrote down a few scriptures from the Bible and advised her that if she paid the truths of these verses a great deal of attention to how she thinks, her attitude would surely change. He informed her that it would undoubtedly improve confidence and faith and return her to health. She was not at all interested. There is unusual mental morbidity in many people who seem to love being miserable and sad.

WHY CHOOSE UNHAPPINESS?

Many people seek to be unhappy by imagining these scenarios: "Today is a black day; everything will go wrong." "I am not going to succeed." "Everyone is against me." "Business is bad, and it is going to get worse." "I am always late." "I never get good breaks." "He can, but I cannot."

If you are stuck in this mental attitude, you will draw all of these thoughts to you and be dissatisfied with life. You must recognize that the world you live in and your mental state are determined mainly by the ideas circulating inside your head. The great Roman philosopher and sage, Marcus Aurelius, declared, "A man's life is what his thoughts make of it." Emerson, a most famous American philosopher, stated, "A man is what he thinks all day long," which couldn't be closer to the truth. The thoughts you regularly entertain within your mind manifest in your physical circumstances. Be sure not to engage in negative thoughts, feelings, or depressing, unkind thoughts. Keep in mind that you can experience no external experience.

IF I HAD A MILLION DOLLARS, I WOULD BE HAPPY

I know about several patients in mental institutions who were millionaires. However, they maintained that they were poor and desperate for money. They were in prison because of schizophrenia, paranoia, and manic depressive tendencies. In and of itself, wealth does not guarantee happiness. However, it is also not a factor that hinders enjoyment, either. Many people are trying to purchase happiness by buying more extensive television sets, fancy sound systems, several cars, homes in both the city and countryside, or even a yacht for private use; however, happiness cannot be acquired in this manner.

True happiness lies in your mind and your feelings. Many people believe that doing something artificial to bring happiness is necessary. Many say, "If I were elected mayor, made president of the organization, promoted to general manager of the corporation, etc., then I would be happy." Happiness is a spiritual and mental state. None of the positions listed can guarantee happiness. Your power, joy, and happiness come only from discovering the laws of divine order and the correct actions that are firmly ingrained in your subconscious mind and implementing these principles in the thoughts and actions of your daily life.

HE FOUND HAPPINESS TO BE THE HARVEST OF A QUIET MIND

While teaching at Munich Academy some years ago, I had the opportunity to interview a man who was extremely unhappy and despaired over how his company was performing. It was his job as the General Manager to bring success to the company. His heart was full of bitterness towards the vice-president and the head of the business. He claimed they were against him remaining in his position. Due to this internal strife, the company suffered, and the man was also not receiving dividends or stock-based bonuses.

Here is how he dealt with his business dilemma. Each day, first thing in the morning, he said, "Everyone who works within our company is honest, genuine, cooperative, loyal, faithful, and of goodwill to everyone. They are both spiritual and mental elements in our company's development chain, including its welfare and prosperity. I radiate peace, love, and goodwill through my words, thoughts, and actions to my two high-level coworkers and everyone else in the company. God guides the president and vice president of our company in their endeavors. My infinitely intelligent subconscious mind makes every decision through me. Only correct and positive action will occur in connection with our business dealings and our relationships with one another. I invite these messages of peace, love, and goodwill to accompany me to the office. Harmony and peace reign in the hearts and minds of everyone within the organization, including myself. I now embark on an exciting new day, full of confidence, faith, and positivity."

The business executive repeated this same meditation slowly three times during the morning and was able to feel the truth of what he believed. When angry or fearful thoughts entered his mind throughout the day, he would say to himself, "Peace, harmony, and poise govern my mind at all times." In disciplining his mind this way, all negative thoughts ceased, and peace flooded his mind.

In the following days, he wrote to me to say that, after around two weeks of organizing his thoughts, the president and vice president sat him down in the office and praised his work and new innovative ideas. They even commented that they were fortunate to have him as their general manager. He was delighted to find out that happiness could be found in himself.

THE BLOCK OR STUMP IS NOT THERE

A few years ago, I read a newspaper article that mentioned a horse that shied away when he approached a stump along the road. Then, each time the horse came across the same stump, it repeated the same fearful action. The farmer dug the stump up, then burned it and leveled the old road. However, for the next 25 years, he shook his head nervously whenever the horse walked by the spot where the stump used to be. The horse was afraid of the idea of an old stump.

Nothing can hinder your happiness except for your mind and mental images. Do you feel that worry or fear is hindering your progress? The thought of fear is what runs through your head. It is possible to remove it in the present moment by replacing it with deep confidence in the possibility of victory, success, and triumph over all obstacles. I was acquainted with a man who was unsuccessful in his business. He told me, "I made a few mistakes. I have learned many things. I am going to return to business and believe I will become a massive success." He stepped past the "stump" of failure in his head. He did not whine or complain. Instead, he removed all thoughts of the possibility of failure, and by believing that his inner power would sustain him, he shook off any fearful thoughts and old demons. Trust in yourself, and you will succeed and be content.

THE HAPPIEST PEOPLE

The happiest man constantly brings forth and implements what is most desirable from within. Virtue and happiness complement one another. Being the very best does not equate with being the happiest, but the most comfortable are typically the most effective at living a life of success. God is the most heavenly and most beautiful thing within you. If you become more of a reflection of God's light, love, truth, and beauty, you will become one of the happiest people around the globe.

Epictetus, a stoic Greek philosopher, stated, "There is but one way to tranquility of mind and happiness; let this, therefore, be always ready at hand with thee, both when thou wakest early in the morning, and all the day long, and when thou goest late to sleep, to account no external things in own but commit all these to God."

SUMMARY OF STEPS TO HAPPINESS

William James said that the most important discovery of this century is the strength of the mind influenced by faith. There is a tremendous strength within you. Pure joy will be there for you once you achieve incredible confidence that you have this ability. **Then,** you can achieve your goals.

You can overcome any obstacle and fulfill your heart's desires by harnessing the remarkable ability of the subconscious. This extraordinary ability is available to anyone who trusts in the Lord's spiritual rules of your subconscious mind and seeks to become happy.

Happiness is a choice you must make. Happiness is an ongoing habit.

It is a better idea to reflect on whatever things are true, whatever things are fair, whatever things are pure, whatever things are beautiful, and whatever things are in good taste. If there is any virtue and any praise, consider these things. Phil. 4:8.

When you wake up at dawn, repeat to yourself: "I will choose happiness today. I am choosing success today. I am making the right decision today. I will choose peace and love for everyone today. I am choosing peace today." Put love, life, and passion into this affirmation, and you have chosen happiness.

Thank God for all of your blessings every day. Also, ask for peace, happiness, and prosperity for your family, friends, and everyone else.

You have to want to be content. There is no way to be fulfilled without first having passion. It is a desire carried on by imagination and fueled by belief. Imagine realizing your wish for happiness and experiencing its completion, then it will come to be. Happiness is found in a prayer answered.

When you constantly dwell on thoughts of anxiety, fear, anger, hatred, or failure, you will soon become depressed and miserable. Remember that your life is the result of what you make it. Make it good.

It is impossible to buy happiness, regardless of how much money you may have at your disposal. Some millionaires are content, while others are desperately unhappy. Many people who have nothing through material possessions are pleased, while others are depressed. Certain married people are satisfied, while others are distraught. A few singles are happy, while some are depressed and lonely. The kingdom of happiness is built within your thoughts and feelings.

Happiness is the result of a calm mind. Concentrate your thoughts on maintaining a sense of calm, tranquility, security.

Since the divine direction and your mind will be a source of joy.

There is no barrier to your happiness. External factors are not the cause of content or discontent. They are just results, not causes. Learn from the sole creative force inside you. Your thoughts are the cause, and each new cause creates a unique effect. Choose to be happy.

The happiest man is the one who can bring out the best in himself and others. God is the highest and best character image because God's kingdom and God himself are inside him.

USE YOUR SUBCONSCIOUS MIND FOR FORGIVENESS

Life plays no favorites. God is life, and the life principle runs through you at all times, including right now. God likes to express Himself in harmony, peace, joy, beauty, and prosperity through you. It is known as"the will" of God or the inclination of life.

If you build up barriers in your mind against the flow of life around your body, this emotional commotion can snarl your mind's subconscious and create unfavorable circumstances. God is not involved with the chaotic or unhappy conditions in the world. It is man's destructive and harmful thinking that designs and builds upon all of the world's problems. It is not a good idea to blame God for your problems or illness or those faced by another.

Many people regularly create mental obstacles to the flow of life by blaming and rebuking God for the sins and sickness of humanity. Some blame God for their suffering or aches, the loss of beloved family members or friends, personal tragedies, and even accidents. They feel angry with God and believe that He is the cause of their miseries.

If people generate and cling to these negative thoughts concerning God, they will feel the pressure of automatic adverse reactions in their minds. In reality, they are unaware that they are putting themselves in harm's way. However, they need to realize the truth to find relief. They must let go of any form of resentment, blame, or anger toward anyone, including God and themselves. If they do not, they will not move toward the successful pursuit of happiness. Alternatively, the very opposite will happen, assuming they can imagine an image of God full of affection and love in their hearts and minds and believe that God is their loving Father watching over them, taking care of them, guiding them, nourishing, and building them up. Those who accomplish this belief in God or the universal power are accepted within their subconscious minds, and they will be blessed in many ways.

LIFE IS ALL-FORGIVING

Life will always forgive. Life will forgive you if you scratch your finger. Your subconscious mind is quick to fix the damage. New cells create bridges across the wound. If you consume poisoned food, life will forgive you and cause you to reject it to safeguard your body's integrity. If your hand is burned, the life principle eases the swelling and provides new skin, tissues, and cells. Trust that life is never avenging you and is always willing to forgive you. Life restores you to peace, health, and vitality when you are in harmony with the natural world. Painful memories, anger, and illness can clog up your thoughts and hinder the flow of the life principle in you. Allow yourself to be forgiven.

HOW HE BANISHED THAT FEELING OF GUILT

I know a colleague who worked in the agency as a Creative Director. He always worked late hours, also on weekends. He remained at work all evening until around 1 a.m. Because of his schedule, he did not pay much attention to his two boys or his spouse. He was always doing his work. He didn't feel he was doing anything wrong externally and expected people to congratulate him with a pat on the back because he worked so hard and remained on-duty past midnight each night. However, he had developed high blood pressure was filled with internal guilt.

He could not stop himself from this pattern and proceeded to punish himself with this grueling schedule and hard work, ignoring those who needed his attention and affection. Ordinary men do not behave like this. It is unhealthy. NormalOrdinary men are interested in their children and their growth and do not keep their wives banished from their lives.

While talking to the man, I explained why I felt the man was working so hard by saying, "Something is eating you from the inside. If it were not, you would not be acting in this manner. You are putting yourself in a bad position and must accept the forgiveness of yourself." As it turns out, he did feel an overwhelming feeling of guilt. It was not even connected to his wife or children, but rather towards someone else. Then, I told him God did not punish him and that he was only being punished by himself and the laws of nature.

If, for instance, you violate the laws of nature, then you will suffer to some extent. If you touch your fingers to a wire with an electric charge, you will get burned. Nature's forces are not evil, but your usage of them will determine whether they have a positive or negative impact. Electricity is not harmful in and of itself. However, the results of using these forces are contingent upon how you use them, whether to torch down a structure or brighten up your home. The only true crime is not knowing the law, and the only sanction is the inevitable consequence of man's infractions against and disregard for the rules of law.

If you make a mistake in connection with the concept of chemistry, it could explode the office or factory. If you knock your hand against aboard, it could cause a wound to your hand. The board is not intended for this purpose. Its proper function may act as a location to lean or assist you to your feet.

During this discussion, the man realized that God does not condemn or punish anyone. He also discovered that he was suffering due to his subconscious mind's response to harmful and destructive thought patterns. He had betrayed his brother once, and the brother had died. He was still overwhelmed with guilt and remorse.

I asked him, "Would you cheat?"

He replied, "No."

"Did you feel you were correct at the time?"

He responded, "Yes."

"But, you would not do it now?"

He said, "No, for now, I am helping others to know how to live."

I nodded and added the following, "You have a greater reason and a deeper understanding of life today. Forgiveness means to accept forgiveness for yourself. To forgive is to align your thoughts with the law of harmony that is divine. Self-condemnation can be described as hell (bondage and restraint). Forgiveness is referred to as heaven (harmony and peace)."

The weight of his guilt was removed from his thoughts, and he could experience total healing. The doctor examined his blood pressure at his next visit, which was expected. The reason for this was the cure. It turned out to be a blessing for his loved ones as well. He enjoyed his family's company as a loving husband and father for the first time in years. The burden of guilt was removed.

A MURDERER LEARNED TO FORGIVE HIMSELF

A man who had killed his brother in Europe came to visit a therapist. He was in a state of anxiety and suffering, believing that God would punish him. He said that his brother was engaged to be married and had his whole life before him, but the man had shot him in the heat of the moment during a dispute. The incident occurred about fifteen years before the interview was conducted with him. This man had been married to an American girl and blessed with three beautiful children in the past. The man lived in an area where he could help many people, becoming a better man with time. He was deeply remorseful.

The therapist explained to the man that psychologically and physically, he was no longer the same person who had killed his brother, as scientists have determined that each cell in our body changes after 11 months. Furthermore, spiritually and mentally, the man had become much different from him at the shooting. Now, he was filled with compassion and goodwill towards humanity. The "old" man who had committed the crime fifteen years earlier was spiritually and mentally dead. In reality, he was pleading for forgiveness as an innocent person!

The explanation profoundly impacted him, and he claimed it was like an enormous weight had been lifted from his life and mind. He was able to see the significance of this verse from the Bible: "Come now, let us think together, says the Lord. If your sins are red, they will be as white as snow. Although they are red like crimson, they will be like wool." ISAIAH 1:18.

CRITICISM CAN NOT HURT YOU WITHOUT YOUR CONSENT

In a letter from one of her students, a teacher was critiqued upon her delivered speech. The student told her that she spoke too fast, which swallowed some of her remarks. The student also indicated that the teacher was too soft-spoken and couldn't be heard, her diction was poor, and her speech sounded unprofessional. The teacher was furious and full of anger towards her critic.

When we first spoke, the teacher refused to acknowledge that her criticisms were valid. While this initial reaction was childish, she later agreed that this letter was beneficial and an excellent correction. She immediately took steps to improve her weaknesses in public speaking by enrolling in a course at City College. She eventually wrote and thanked the author of the note for his feedback, which had allowed the teacher to fix the problem immediately.

HOW TO BE COMPASSIONATE

If only none of the points stated in the letter were valid for the teacher, her response might have been very different. The teacher would likely be immediately aware of the incorrect accusations of faulty speaking and not respond with the anger she had initially felt. Instead, she would probably have acknowledged that her classes had somehow upset the student critic's beliefs prejudices or went against her narrow religious doctrines. Moreover, the student could have suffered from psychological illness, causing her to express anger over something seemingly trivial, which could have led the teacher, potentially, to respond with compassion rather than anger and then acceptance.

Understanding this type of reaction and not judging or becoming angry means showing compassion. The next step is a prayer for the other person's peace, harmony, and understanding. You are not at risk since you realize that you control your reactions, thoughts, and feelings. Emotions accompany thoughts, and you possess the ability to block all ideas that could cause you to become disturbed or angry.

LEFT AT THE ALTAR

A few years ago, I learned about a marriage ceremony. Surprisingly, the man who was set to marry did not show up at the ceremony location. After waiting until the end of the two hours that had been scheduled for the ceremony, the bride shed a few tears, then said, "I prayed for divine guidance. It could be the answer since He never fails."

This was her beautiful response—faith in God and everything good. There was no bitterness in her soul over the situation, and she said, "Marriage must not have been the right action because my prayer was for right action for both of us." Another person who had faced similar circumstances would have likely left the establishment in a rage, been brought to a state of emotional turmoil, required sedation, and reasonably possibly required hospitalization due to this level of emotional trauma.

Be aware of the endless wisdom that lies within your subconscious. Believe in the answers you receive in the same way you loved your mom when she held you in her arms— unconditional love and belief that everything is correct. This is the way you improve your mental and emotional well-being.

IT IS WRONG TO MARRY. SEX IS EVIL. I AM EVIL.
A true story about an unidentified young woman who was twenty-two years old: she was taught that it was sinful to dance, play cards, swim, and go out with males, among other things. Her mother threatened her, stating that she would be burned forever in hellfire if she did not obey her maternal wishes and belief system. The girl had always worn a black dress with black stockings. She did not put on lipstick, rouge, or any other form of makeup as her mother indicated that such items were considered illegal. Additionally, she had been taught that everyone was evil and that sex was the devil's work and a form of extreme debauchery.

The girl lived her life with an overwhelming sense of guilt over her head at all times. She lost her sense of self in following her mother's wishes. To move forward, she had to shed the false notions that ruled her life and embrace the reality of the world in which she lived. She also needed to build a new perception of herself. Obstacles were plenty during this time of growth. When she was with young men at the office where she worked, she felt overwhelming guilt and believed God would punish her. Several eligible young men even proposed to her, but she declined. She told me, "It is not right to get married. Sexuality is sinful, and I am inherently evil." Her "conscience" speaking was also known as her early training. Unfortunately, it was highly misguided.

Luckily she met a therapist and saw him once a week for about ten weeks; she met a therapist and saw for about ten weeks once a week. She was instructed about the functions of the unconscious and conscious mind. The young woman slowly realized that she was utterly obsessed, brainwashed, and conditioned by a naïve, superstitious, and angry mother. It was only then that she could walk away from her parents.

She began living a lavish life, following my suggestion that she make up for the lost time by getting dressed up in fashions she loved and having her hair styled in ways that made her feel beautiful. She learned to dance with a man who also gave her driving lessons. She soon learned to swim, play cards, and go on multiple dates. She sought a divine partner, claiming the Infinite Spirit would draw to her the man of her dreams, one who matched with her entirely and perfectly. In the end, this is precisely what happened. One evening, another individual was waiting to meet the therapist when she left his office, and he informally introduced them. They have now been married for many years and complement one another perfectly!

FORGIVENESS IS NECESSARY FOR HEALING

"When you pray, be kind to yourself, even if you have a right to do so against anyone." MARK 11:25.

Forgiving others is vital for your peace of mind and glowing health. You must forgive everyone you have ever been wronged by if you desire a perfect state of health and happiness. Let yourself forgive yourself by keeping your thoughts aligned with the divine law and order. You cannot truly be forgiven entirely until you have forgiven other people first. The refusal to forgive yourself is no less than spiritual arrogance or ignorance.

In psychosomatic medicine, anger, resentment, denial of others' actions, guilt, and hostility cause various ailments ranging from arthritis to heart disease. They say that the injured, mistreated, deceived, or wounded patients were filled with hate and resentment towards those who hurt them. It led to a resurgence of injuries in their minds. There is only one solution. It is necessary to eliminate their pain, and the most reliable and secure way is to get them to forgive themselves and others.

FORGIVENESS IS LOVE IN ACTION

The most critical component of forgiveness is the desire to accept it fully. If you genuinely want to forgive someone else, you are already 51 percent of the way to the goal. I am sure you realize that forgivingignoring someone else does not necessarily mean you must love him or wish to get to know him. There is no obligation to be a fan of someone. Neither is a government able to regulate love, goodwill, or peace. It is impossible to love someone simply because somebody in Washington issues an order to this effect, but it *is* possible to be a lover of people without liking them.

The Bible states, love each other. Anyone can do that if they so desire. The word "love" means you wish for their peace, health, happiness, joy, and that they are blessed with all the good things in life. There is just one condition for this love to be accurate, sincerity. You must want this for the other person. If you are not generous when you accept forgiveness, you are selfish. What you wish for someone else is something you also want for yourself. Is there anything more simple than this?

TECHNIQUE OF FORGIVENESS

The following is an essential technique connected with forgiveness that will work miracles in your life if and when you apply it: Clear your mind. Just let it go free. Imagine God and His unconditional love for you. Then declare, "I fully and freely accept forgiveness (mention your name and the identity of the person who has offended). I let him and his actions go both spiritually and mentally. I forgive all that is associated with the subject. I am completely free, and so is he. It is a wonderful feeling. Today is my day of total amnesty. I release anyone and everyone whom I have ever hurt. I wish all people peace, happiness, health, and all of the joys that life can offer. I do this without cost—

joyfully and with love." Then, when you take a moment to think about the individual or people who have hurt me, affirm, "I have let you go, and all the blessings in the world are now yours. You are free, and you are free. It is wonderful!"

The secret to true forgiveness is that it is unnecessary to make a new prayer after granting it. If the subject comes to your thoughts, or if the specific hurt crosses your mind, you should wish the person who has offended you well and then say, "Peace be with you." Repeat this repeatedly as soon as the thought comes into your mind. It will be apparent that the idea of the incident or person will gradually fade away. It will come less and less frequently and eventually fade into obscurity.

THE ACID TEST FOR FORGIVENESS

Gold is tested with acid. There is also an acid test to determine forgiveness. If I share something positive about someone who has offended you, cheated you, or defrauded you, and you squeal or wince after hearing the positive news. The underlying causes of hate remain within your mind's subconscious, wreaking havoc on your health and wellbeing.

Let us say you suffered an abscess on your jaw about a year ago and had told me about it. I would then casually ask whether you were experiencing any discomfort today. You would automatically answer, "Of course not; I have a memory of it but no more pain." This is the complete story of how you must feel when forgiving someone. There may be a recollection of the incident, but you do not feel any pain or sting anymore. It is the test you must pass, and you must give the challenge spiritually and psychologically; otherwise, you are just faking it and not pursuing the actual practice of forgiving.

TO UNDERSTAND ALL IS TO FORGIVE ALL

If a person can comprehend the law of creation in his mind, he will stop blaming other people or circumstances for causing harm or affecting his life. He realizes that his thoughts alone determine the destiny of his life. Additionally, he realizes that external influences are not the main factors that shape his life and experiences. If you think that other people can ruin your happiness, which is why you are the victim of a terrible fate, you will spend your entire life fighting against others. This idea is unjustified once you realize that thoughts determine all things. The Bible affirms the same. "If a man thinks in his mind and acts in his heart, so is the man." PROVERBS 23:7.

SUMMARY OF YOUR AIDS TO FORGIVENESS

God or Life plays no favorites. God or Life appears to favor you when you are aligned with the principles of harmony, health, joy, and peace.

God or Life does not send sickness, disease, or pain. We create these conditions through our own destructive beliefs based on the law, just as we reap what we sow.

Your perception of God will be the main crucial factor in your life. **If you genuinely believe in the God who loves you, then your mind will send out a multitude of blessings for you. Believe in the existence of a God that is love.**

Life or God has no grudges against you. Life never condemns you. Energy can heal a severe cut to your finger. The universe forgives you when the finger is burned because of your carelessness. It minimizes the edema and returns the area to its fullness and perfection.

Your guilt-based mentality is a false notion based on a flawed concept of God and Life. God or Life is not a punisher, nor do they decide on your behalf. You are doing this to yourself through wrong beliefs, negative thinking, and self-condemnation.

God or Life does not judge and punish you. Nature's forces are not evil. The impact of their application depends on the method you employ to harness the power that is within you. It is possible to use electricity to kill someone or provide light to your home. Water can be used to drown children or quench their thirst. The distinction between good and evil goes back to thought and motives in man's mind.

God or Life does not punish. Man is punished by his false beliefs about God, Life, and the Universe. Man's thoughts are creative, and he causes the circumstances that cause him to suffer.

If you are the victim of criticism, and the faults are your own, then rejoice in the guidance, offer gratitude, and thank them for the feedback. This will give you a valuable opportunity to fix the issue.

You are not harmed by criticism when you realize that you are in control of your thoughts, your reactions, and even your emotions. This allows you to pray and bless others by blessing yourself.

If you ask for direction and the right course of action, follow the path that comes. Be aware that it is highly excellent. There is no reason for self-pity, criticism, or resentment.

Nothing is good or bad, except how you think establishes it as one or another. There is nothing wrong with sexuality or sex, the desire to eat, wealth, or any true expression. It is all in how you respond to these desires, urges, or aspirations. The desire to eat can be fulfilled without killing anyone for a loaf of bread.

Resentment, anger, hatred, ill-will, and hostility can be the source of numerous ailments. You can forgive yourself and others by offering happiness, joy, love, and peace to all the people who have caused you pain. Keep doing this until you have them in your thoughts and are at peace with them.

The word "forgive" means to provide something. Give peace, love, happiness, wisdom, joy, and all the good things in life to another until there is no trace of sting left in your heart. It is the actual test for forgiveness.

Let us suppose that you suffered an abscess inside your jaw around one year ago. It was excruciating. Consider whether it is hurting right now. It is negative. Similarly, if someone injured you, deceived you, or slandered you and you aimed to forgive them, is your perception of the person you are thinking about still negative? Do you get a glimmer of anger whenever they come to your thoughts? If yes, the seeds of hate are still present, inflicting havoc on you and your well-being. The only way to deal with this is to continue to treat them with kindness by offering them all happiness in life. It will take time until you can meet them in your thoughts and respond with a prayer of peace and goodwill.

CLEANSE YOUR MIND

My soul is filled with divine love. Achieving the divine right action is my responsibility. Religious harmony rules my life.

Heavenly peace fills my soul. The beauty of God is mine. Great joy fills my heart. God guides me in all directions. I am illuminated from God on high. I believe and know that I will be blessed with an abundance of love, including beauty, truth, and honesty greater than my most ardent dreams. I am confident that universal love and kindness will surround me.

Commentary: Life in the modern world is chaotic and filled with irrelevant distractions and worries. If you feel uncomfortable by the demands of life, spend some time to settle your thoughts and remember that you are designed to be joyful.

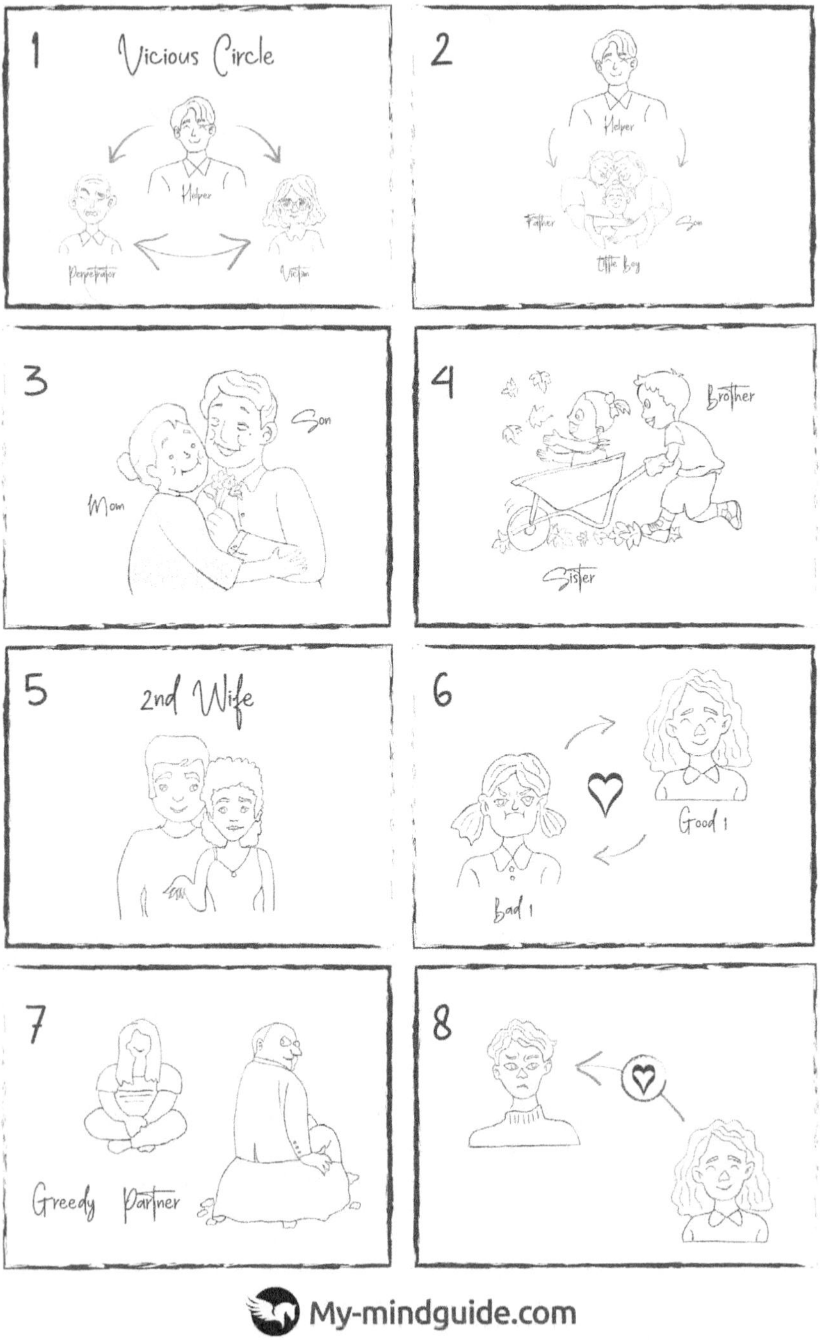
1
Vicious Circle
Helper
Perpetrator
Victim
2
Helper
Father
Son
Little Boy
3
Son
Mom
4
Brother
Sister
5
2nd Wife
6
Good 1
Bad 1
7
Greedy
Partner
8

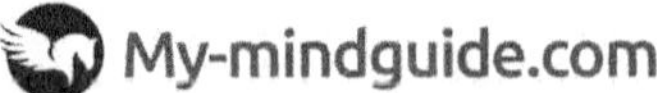

AFFIRM THE POWER OF YOUR SUBCONSCIOUS MIND

I can accomplish everything by the power in my unconscious mind. Whatever thoughts I subconsciously impress onto my subconscious will develop an avenue to bring them to life. Health, strength, and goodwill are a constant source of inspiration for my friends, family members, and myself. I wish the best to every person I meet every day. I am grateful for the many good fortunes bestowed upon me.

Commentary: To allow positive affirmations to have any effect, they must be convinced of the power of faith. Affirmations help build the belief that acts as the basis that all subsequent assertions are constructed.

ASSIGN YOUR CONSCIOUS MIND THE ROLE OF GATEKEEPER

My conscious mind is the guard on the other side of the fence, securing my thoughts from false perceptions. It denies any thoughts that are not in line with the universal rules of love, health, wisdom, and prosperity. It snuffs out any ideas which could undermine my self-esteem. I am who I think I am and want to be, and through my mind's eye, I have complete influence over my thoughts. I can choose to think of joy, peace, and health and believe in a love that is abundant and available to everyone.

Commentary: You might not control what happens to you throughout your life, but you do have complete control over what you feel about it. A person or an event cannot cause you to feel angry, depressed, or bitter. You can feel jealous, angry, or insecure, but if you allow it to, your conscious mind will protect you from such thoughts by refusing to accept them. It is the gatekeeper.

EMBRACE AND EMBODY TRUTH

God's love, truth, and wisdom fill my mind and my heart. I believe in the fact. I am aware of the truth. God's peace-filled river overflows my mind, and I am grateful for my liberation. I am a righteous thinker as I reflect the divine wisdom of God and his divine insight in all aspects. My brain is the mind of God that is unchanging and forever. I recognize God's voice. God has the power of peace, honesty, and love. My mind is filled with God's wisdom and knowledge. Today, everything bothering me is gone, and I am free and in peace.

Commentary: Deceit, lies, misinformation, half-truths, and false notions are the primary causes of much human suffering because they create distorted thinking. God is the only truth, and to be one to God can be described as being in complete alignment with the truth. If you do not embrace and live in fact, you will be at odds with it and, therefore, prone to suffering from all kinds of unfortunate events.

IDENTIFY YOUR LIFE'S PURPOSE

My unconscious mind's infinity shows me my identity in this world. I follow its direction, which can be seen in my conscious mind logically. It has a deep understanding of me. It knows my preferences, interests, knowledge, and talents and provides me with opportunities that I am well-suited to and fascinated by. I am open to those opportunities and realize that I am content and productive at work. I am at peace with my coworkers and supervisors, enabling us to reach our shared objectives. I add value and creatively utilize my brain to develop innovative ideas for services, products, and processes. Moreover, I have compensated accordingly.

Commentary: Most people want to live a "purpose-driven life," but many are not sure of their goal in life or for what they should strive for. This affirmation can help you transmit the problem to your subconscious mind—the imaginative part of your brain which acts as a portal to infinite wisdom. It is your perfect positioning service, and it will find your ideal position and the most suitable match for you.

RECEIVE THE PERFECT PLAN

The infinite wisdom that brought me this dream guides me and shows me the ideal strategy for realizing the dream. I recognize that the more excellent intuition within my mind is responding. What I experience and believe within can be expressed in the absence. I will have balance, equilibrium, and a sense of peace in my daily life.

Commentary: Your conscious brain is rational, whereas the subconscious is imaginative and intuitive. Your subconscious mind will be impressed by everything you wish for in life, and it will develop an idea and draw in all the resources necessary to accomplish the result of your dreams or the goal you want to achieve.

The thought of planning can affect the functioning of your unconscious mind. Send your desires into your mind's subconscious and let it perform its work. If you let the subconscious think it, it can often lead to the perfect idea; it will appear in a "flash of genius" with minimal effort.

LIVE A HARMONIOUS LIFE

Infinite intelligence guides and leads me through all my paths. My perfect health is mine, as the law of harmony operates in my body and mind. Peace, beauty, love, and prosperity are my own. The principles of correct action and divine law govern my life. I am aware that my primary basis is founded on the timeless facts of life. I feel, know, and believe that my unconscious mind reacts by the character of my conscious brain.

Commentary: While sure scientists believe there is chaos in our universe, it is, in reality, well-ordered and controlled by laws. Natural laws govern the physical universe. Likewise, moral rules determine the behavior of humans. Being in accord with these timeless rules will bring wealth, health, peace, happiness, and harmony. This general statement puts you in the direction of living a harmonious life.

SLEEP IN PEACE AND WAKE IN JOY

My toes are in a relaxed state, my ankles are in a relaxed state, and the abdominal muscles of my body are at ease. My lungs and heart are at ease. My arms and hands are at ease, my neck is comfortable, my brain is calm, my face is relaxed, my eyes are relaxed, and my body and mind are in a state of relaxation. I wholly and freely forgive anyone and would like peace, harmony, health, and prosperity. I am calm, at peace, serene. I feel secure and safe. Profound stillness embraces me, and a deep peace relaxation fills my entire being when I recognize that it is God who surrounds me. I know that the realization of love and life is healing for me. I take a deep breath and wrap myself in the robe of love before falling asleep filled with goodwill for all. Peace is still with me through the night, and when I wake up, I will be full of life and love.

Commentary: If you have insomnia, you will use this affirmation positively, as many people have before. Repeat it slowly, calmly, and lovingly before going to bed. There is no need for any additional sleep aids.

MAKE HAPPINESS A HABIT

Divine order rules my day today. All things are working together for the best outcomes for me. It is a brand new and exciting moment. There will not ever be another day like this. God guides me throughout the day, and all that I do will succeed. God's love surrounds me and envelopes me. I walk forward in tranquility. If my attention drifts away from the sound and constructive things, I will immediately return it to the focus of all that is wonderful and of good character. I am a mental and spiritual magnet, attracting myself to all things that will bless and benefit me. I am going to achieve great success in my endeavors today. I will be content all day long.

Commentary: A few years ago, I was able to stay for about a week at the home of a farmer in rural Upper Austria. He was always singing and whistling and seemed filled with laughter. I asked him about the key to his happiness, and his answer is "It has become a routine of mine to be content. Every morning, when I wake up and before I go to bed, I pray for my family, my crops, my cattle, and thanks to God for the amazing harvest."

The farmer made this practice a habit for more than forty years. It is well-known that repeated thoughts frequently and regularly become a part of the subconscious mind and eventually become routines. Happiness is a habit.

CLAIM A BETTER FUTURE

I am filled with the energizing cleansing, healing, revitalizing, and harmonizing power of The Holy Spirit. My body is the dwelling place of the living God and is clean, complete, whole, and flawless in every aspect. Every part of my body and mind is controlled through divine guidance. I look toward a spectacular future. I am in the blissful anticipation of the very most beautiful times to come. The God-like thoughts that I have today are absorbed into my subconscious mind, like seeds planted in fertile soil. I am confident that when their time has arrived, they will spring forth in peace, harmony, health, and opportunity, as well as providing extraordinary experiences and even events.

I am now free from fear and apathy, living a life of freedom through God. God is rising within me. Behold! I create all things new!

Commentary: Every day is a new one for renewal and rebirth. Every aspect of nature proclaims the glory of a brand new day. It is the reason to remind ourselves to be awakened by God inside us, rise from our winter-like slumber of limitations, and step into the dawn of a brand new day and a new life. The fear of ignorance, anxiety, and superstition should be gone in us, and we must bring back faith and love in its place. Start now to receive the blessing of God's love and grace through this affirmation.

CURE YOURSELF

My body and its organs were designed by the infinite wisdom of my unconscious mind. It can help me heal. Its understanding created my tissues, organs, bones, and muscles. The healing force inside me transforms every atom of me to make me complete and whole. I am grateful for the healing that I am sure is happening through the works of the creative genius inside me.

Commentary: Your subconscious has initiated your heartbeat, regulates the flow of blood, and controls the processes of digestion, respiration, and elimination. If you consume a slice of bread, your unconscious brain transforms it into muscle, tissue, blood, and bone. It is responsible for all essential processes and functions that your body performs. If your unconscious mind could create you from scratch, it can undoubtedly cure you and free you from disease. You change your body when you alter your thoughts by immersing them in endless affirmations. It is the essence of the healing process in general.

HEAL OTHERS REMOTELY

The healing power is where _______ is. The physical state of her body is an expression of her thoughts. I am aware that I need to alter my projection device to change the image on the screen. The projection reel is my mind. I am now projecting in my mental image the picture of completeness, harmony, peace, and total health for ____________. The eternal healing power that gave birth to __________'s body and organs is infiltrating every atom of her, acting as a stream that peacefully flows throughout each cell in her body. Doctors are guided by God and directed to heal. Anyone who comes in contact with ________ is urged to act in the best way. I am aware that illness is not a reality in itself. I am now aligned to the universal idea of love and living, and know and affirm peace and harmony are currently being manifested in the body of _____________.

Commentary: Infinite Intelligence flows throughout everything and is not confined by space or time. It is the source of phenomena like psychic telepathy, extrasensory perception, astral projection, and the healing power of prayer. It is the key to unlimited intelligence, allowing you to tap into its ability to heal people, whether near, across town, or even halfway around the globe.

Be aware that negative thoughts can also be transmitted through the internet and harm others. Positive thoughts, just like positive acts, are valuable contributions to society. Thoughts that are destructive, similar to violent actions, can damage the community.

ATTRACT MONEY

I am a fan of money. I love it, and I utilize it responsibly in a constructive, judicious, and responsible manner. Money is continuously circulating throughout my life. I let it go with joy, and it comes back to me in a beautiful way. The cash flows into me in vast swathes of wealth. I only use it to benefit myself and others, and I am thankful for the blessings of my life and the abundance of my thoughts.

Commentary: The goal of the principle of life is to drive you toward expansion, growth, and making life more enjoyable. It is not your intention to live in a slum or dress in rags and be hungry. You are supposed to be content, prosperous, successful, and wealthy. Do not criticize the wealth of others or people who have plenty. Get rid of any weird and superstitious ideas regarding money. Do not ever think of money as filthy or evil. When you feel that way, it will allow it to take wings and take flight away from you. You lose what you criticize. It is impossible to attract attention to the things you denigrate.

SECURE A CONSTANT SUPPLY OF MONEY

I am one with endless wealth in my unconscious mind. My right is to live with great wealth while being happy and prosperous. The money flows freely to me constantly, in copious amounts, and forever. I am always aware of my value. I utilize my talents to the best of my incredible abilities, and I am fortunate financially. It is amazing!

Commentary: Recognizing the power that your mind's subconscious has, as well as the creativity of your mental images or thoughts, can lead to freedom, opulence, and an endless supply of cash. Be grateful for the abundance of life that is within your mind. Your acceptance of your mind and the expectation of wealth have their mechanics and expression mathematics. If you can adopt the attitude of opulence, everything essential to live a whole and abundant life will begin to manifest. Make this your daily affirmation. Write it on your heart.

PROSPER IN ALL OF YOUR INTERESTS

In the daytime and at night, I am prospering in all areas of my life.

Commentary: Sometimes, a straightforward affirmation is ideal but not overly forceful. In certain instances, it is common for people to affirm their beliefs when the conscious mind denies the statement as false and does not pass it on in the subconscious mind. For example, your subconscious mind might reject the assertion that you have earned millions of dollars. However, it may believe, as an affirmation, that you are wealthy in all of your pursuits. I suggested to a businessman whose sales and financials were in an abysmal state and who was deeply anxious that he lay in his office or a quiet place, take a deep breath and repeat every day: "My sales are improving every day." This simple declaration triggered the brain's conscious and subconscious minds, and the desired outcomes followed.

MAKE WISE FINANCIAL AND INVESTMENT DECISIONS

The infinite intelligence supervises all my financial transactions, and everything I do will be successful.

Commentary: If you are looking for wisdom on investments or are concerned about your stocks and bonds, repeat this affirmation to teach your mind to make wise investment choices. Repeat this often, and you will notice that your investment is prudent and, more importantly, you will be safe from losses as you will be motivated to sell your holdings of securities before any loss arising to your portfolio.

RECOVER FROM A FINANCIAL SETBACK

I have experienced a loss of money. I will get back to work and earn more. I have learned a great lesson, which will yield dividends. I have not lost my faith and confidence or the ability to improve and grow. I have plenty to contribute and can be a massive success once more. God is the primary source of my wealth, and His riches are moving through my life. There is always an abundant divine supply. God shows the way for me to achieve success in the religious order.

Commentary: It is not the outcome that is important. The most important thing is what you think about it and your constructive or destructive response. Use your imagination with care and create a state of mind with a brand new pattern, imagining the future and using the wings of imagination and faith to make a better life. Wealth and success are the results of your thinking and your beliefs.

FIND YOUR IDEAL HOME OR APARTMENT

The infinite wisdom of my subconscious is intelligent and all-knowing. It has revealed that the perfect house, located in a central area and a beautiful setting, fulfills all my needs and is in line with my income. I am currently turning this inquiry to my subconscious mind, and I am confident that it will respond to the specifics of my demand. I make this release with complete faith and trust like farmers who plant seeds in the soil, trusting entirely in the laws of nature.

Commentary: When buying and selling, be aware that the conscious part of your mind starts the process while your unconscious mind acts as the engine. It is essential to start the motor for it to function. The first step in communicating the idea of your desire clearly or creating an image within the more discerning mind is to let it relax and numb the mind while remaining still and calm. A calm, relaxed, and peaceful state of mind keeps out any irrelevant matters and false thoughts, which can hinder your mind's ability to absorb your ideas. In addition, with a calm mind and a receptive and passive attitude, your conscious effort is decreased to a minimal level.

Answers to your question could appear through advertisements in the newspaper or news from a trusted friend. Perhaps you will even be guided directly past a specific home that is precisely what you have been looking for. There are numerous ways to receive an answer in connection with the prayer you have made. The most important thing to know, and where you need to place your trust, is that the answer is always there when you believe in the work of your inner mind.

SELL YOUR HOME OR OTHER PROPERTY

Infinite intelligence draws me to those buyers looking to purchase and thrive in it. The buyers are sent into my life by my subconscious's imaginative brain, which is unwavering. They might look at different homes; however, mine is what they most desire and are most likely to purchase because unlimited wisdom guides them from within. I know that the buyers are correct, the timing is right, and the cost is set correctly. Everything about this is correct. The deepest reaches in my unconscious mind are operating and bringing us into the divine order. I am sure that it is true.

Commentary: Remember that who or what you are looking for is also looking for you. So, if you decide to sell a property or home of any type, there is always someone looking for the things you have to provide. Utilizing the ability of your mind's subconscious effectively, you can rid your mind of all feelings of anxiety and competition in selling or buying.

SOLVE A PROBLEM

My subconscious has the answer. It is responding to me right now. Thank you for the knowledge that the infinity of my subconscious mind is aware of. It knows everything and is providing the perfect solution to me right now. My conviction lies in liberating the power and splendor in my mind's subconscious. I am happy that it is as it should be.

Commentary: People tend to tackle their issues, often creating more problems because of their efforts. Instead of using your conscious mind to solve problems, shift it to the subconscious brain, as it is better equipped to tackle complex issues. Sometimes, your subconscious mind can solve the case with the conscious mind asleep, and you awake knowing the answer.

FIND LOST OR MISPLACED ITEMS

You are aware of everything. You are aware of where __________ is, and you are now revealing to me the exact location.

Commentary: Recite this affirmation many times per day, particularly before going to sleep. Your subconscious knows "the last place you had it." If something has been lost or misplaced, infinite intelligence knows the location and will transmit the details to you via that powerhouse of the subconscious. Your subconscious mind will respond to you if you trust it.

MAKE AN IMPORTANT OR DIFFICULT DECISION

The creative mind of my subconscious knows the best thing for me. Tendencies are always upward, and it helps me make the best decision that benefits everyone involved. I thank God for the solution that I believe will come to me.

Commentary: If you are confronted with an important life choice, such as the decision to switch jobs, relocate, separate, marry, or have children, engage your subconscious. Your rational, conscious mind might be able to think of the best option; however, your gut instinct is likely to guide you to a choice by the divine command: Trust your instincts. A girl living in Los Angeles decided to accept a job in New York City at twice her current salary. The affirmation was repeated several times before sleeping, and the following day, she was afflicted with a strong sense that she could not take the job offer. She turned down the request, and subsequent events confirmed her inner knowing. The company was bankrupt within a short time following the offer of employment. The conscious mind might be right when it comes to objectively facts; however, the intuitive faculties that form her unconscious mind were aware of the impending failure of the business in question, causing her to decide to act accordingly.

LOVE UNCONDITIONALLY

I offer my love free of charge to _______ in exchange for the pleasure and satisfaction of knowing that they will be joyful. My love-giving gift comes with no conditions attached. It is as easy as the breeze. I do not expect anything in return since the ability to be in love and express it is a beautiful benefit in itself. I am grateful for the joy that love can bring to myself and those around me.

Commentary: Too often, we give and love others with expectations of a reward such as gratitude, recognition, requited love, or even future tips. If our expectations are not met, the love we feel turns into anger and bitterness, which can entrap both the giver and the recipient. True love can be liberating. If you decide to give love, do it from your heart and for nothing more than the pleasure and excitement of making others happy and liberated. You will receive many blessings from the giving, but do not give in the hope of receiving these blessings.

FORGIVE OTHERS

I freely and completely forgive ______________. I let the person go free from any ill will, both spiritually and mentally. I completely forgive everything that has to do with the issue in dispute. I am free, and so are they. It is an amazing feeling. It is an amnesty day for me in general. I am releasing everyone and anyone who has hurt me in the past.

Further, I wish for everyone to be blessed with peace, happiness, health, along with all of the good things of life. I do this without any cost, without hesitation, joyfully, and with love. When I think about the person or people who have hurt me, I affirm, "I have released you and pray that all of the joys in the world are yours. You are free, and I can be free. It is wonderful!

Commentary: The essential aspect of genuine forgiveness is that you do not need to repeat the statement once you have accepted the desire to offer forgiveness to someone else. If the subject comes to your thoughts, or the specific incident happens to enter your mind, be sure to wish the offender well, and then say, "Peace be to you." Repeat this every time the thought comes into your mind. After several days, the idea or experience will fade away gradually, appearing in your mindless frequently until it fades to nothingness.

WISH OTHERS WELL

I wish each of us the same things I want for myself: peace, joy, love, and God's abundant blessings. I am elated and grateful for the progress, growth, and prosperity.

Commentary: The most important law is: If you would like others to think about you and wish you well, imagine them in the same way. In the same way, you want others to feel about you, do you think about them in the same way? Never attempt to deprive someone else of the joy that they feel. If you do, you also deny yourself. What you believe to be true for you, make it so for everyone. If you believe in peace and happiness, then let it include peace, joy, and harmony for everyone. When the ship arrives for the human race, it will also come to you.

ATTRACT YOUR SOULMATE

I am currently attracting an honest, genuine, committed, loyal, and happy individual. They are peaceful, content, and prosperous. These traits that I am awestruck by are being absorbed into my mind's subconscious and surfacing in my mind. When I reflect on these traits, they become part of me and are manifested subconsciously. My ideals are dear to them, and I admire their ideals. They do not wish to change me, nor will I ever want to alter them. We share a love for each other, freedom, respect, and love. We are inexplicably attracted to one another. Only what is a part of love, beauty, truth, and truth will come into my world. I am embracing my ideal partner today.

Commentary: You are welcome to edit this affirmation to define what you are looking for more specifically in your ideal partner. Repeat the claim in your daily meditation practice. While you contemplate quietly and with a keen interest in the qualities and traits that appeal to the person you are seeking, you will develop the equivalent mental picture within your mind. Then, your subconscious's more powerful mental tidal waves will bring both of you together in perfect order.

SUPPORT YOUR SPOUSE SPIRITUALLY

I am confident that the person I am with is open to my positive thoughts and images. I affirm, feel, and know that peace is the very core of their existence. God guides my spouse in every way. They are a conduit for God's divine. God's love fills their mind and heart. Peace, harmony, and understanding lie between us. I imagine them as joyful, healthy, happy, and blessed. I surround them in the sacred divine love circle, indestructible, impervious, and unaffected by negative influences.

Commentary: An article by a woman from London claimed that her husband had lost his entire wealth in the stock market and that he was feeling lost and morbidly depressed. He was seeking a divorce and claimed that she was trying to nag to the point of death.

I explained that constantly nagging her spouse was the fastest way to end the marriage. I also told her that this was when he required encouragement and support more than ever. She outlined the positive traits and behaviors he displayed when she married him. I informed her that those characteristics that attracted her to him initially are still present but must be revived. It can be done through affirmations.

I offered her the above affirmation that she could repeat regularly and emphasized how her husband would receive her spiritual guidance subconsciously, and they would be blessed. They discussed this during my trip to London and later agreed to pray together. The husband has recently been offered a lucrative job. Prayer can change things. It alters the person praying and those being prayed for in extraordinarily beneficial ways.

MAINTAIN A STRONG MARRIAGE

The Spirit that is in me talks to the Spirit in ______. Peace, harmony, and love are ours at all times. God speaks, thinks, and acts on my behalf, and God speaks, thinks, and acts through my spouse.

Commentary: One affirmation will not be enough to strengthen the bond between couples. Both partners must maintain positive attitudes towards the other person and show their affection and respect all day long. Alongside saying this affirmation every day, there are five steps to keeping your marriage strong:

1. Do not carry on irritations that arise from minor disappointments from day-to-day. Let each other be forgiven for any harshness before you head off to bed at night.

2. You can be sure that infinite intelligence guides you in all of your choices. Send your positive thoughts of peace and harmony, along with love, to your spouse or partner, to all the family members, and all of the world.

3. Breakfast is a time to be grateful for the fantastic meal, for the abundance of food, and all of your other blessings. Be sure that no issues or arguments take place over the table conversation. The same is true at dinnertime.

4. Speak to your spouse daily and say, "I appreciate all that you are doing, and I radiate love and goodwill to you all day long."

5. Do not give your partner a chance to feel like they are being taken for granted. Show your appreciation and affection often. The best way to create peace in your home and experience an enjoyable marriage is to build the base of harmony, beauty, love, and mutual respect. The relationship should be built upon a foundation of faith and all that is positive.

LET GO OF A TROUBLESOME RELATIONSHIP

I release _______________. They are in the proper position at all times, just like I am. We both have decided to separate and take different routes. I have decided that my words will be poured out to the infinite mind and brought to fruition. It is the way it is.

Commentary: Relationships can be hard to end, particularly in the case of a partner who is not seeking to end the relationship. In these situations, anger and anxiety can be overpowering. The decision to end the relationship and imagining the two of you going in your separate directions sends a clear signal to the world that the relationship has come to an end.

GAIN CLOSURE

It is a perfectly harmonious solution. It was completed according to the divine guidelines.

Commentary: If you are in a stressful situation and can see an end to the problem, consider repeating this affirmation and letting it become your mantra. Believe that "this too shall pass" and leave the infinite wisdom to solve the problem. By making this decision, you let go and relinquish conscious control, thus freeing your mind and allowing it to solve the problem without much effort or stress.

IMPROVE YOUR MEMORY

My memory as of today has improved in every area. I will never forget what I am required to remember at any time or space. The impressions I receive will be more precise and have better precision. I will remember them quickly and effortlessly. What

I need to remember will be immediately in my head correctly. I am getting better each day, and very shortly, my memory will be sharper than ever before.

Commentary: Do not think or speak words such as, "I am losing my memory," or "Maybe I am getting dementia." If those thoughts pass through the security to your subconscious mind and become a part of your subconscious, the subconscious will start to realize those thoughts. Replace negative thoughts by focusing on positive reviews.

BREAK A BAD HABIT

My thoughts are filled with peace, balance, and poise. The endless possibilities lie in the slumber of my soul. I am not scared of any past, present, or future aspect. The infinity that is my unconscious mind directs and guides me in every way. I can now face every challenge with confidence, calmness, and confidence. I am completely free of bad habits. My mind is filled with peace and happiness. I am forgiven, and health, peace, and faith are the top priorities in my life.

Commentary: The human body is a product of habit. Habit is the job that your mind's subconscious performs. You learned to swim, cycle, dance, and drive a vehicle by repeating these actions repeatedly until they carved out a path within your subconscious mind. After that, they became automatic behaviors that your mind's subconscious controlled. This is often referred to as something that becomes 'second nature as it is a response that your unconscious mind has to your thoughts and behavior. It is your choice to make good, bad, correct, or wrong habits. If you repeat a negative review or action for an extended period, you will be stuck in the grip of a habit. The rule of your subconscious is the compulsion.

OVERCOME A BAD TEMPER

From now on, I will become more cheerful. Happiness and joy are becoming my normal mental states. Every day, I am becoming more loveable, loving, and compassionate. I am now the source of joy and kindness to my friends and family by infecting them with my happiness. This positive mood is becoming my normal mental state. I am grateful.

Commentary: If your attitude is typically one that consists of feelings of anger or dislike towards any person, like your neighbors, friends, colleagues, or even your supervisor, you can change your relationship by altering the way you view the person. People become more accomodating when they generally have a more positive outlook on life. It shaped their attitudes towards the people in their lives. Even if things do not change noticeably in the direction you want them to, your positive outlook will help you feel less miserable in the presence of annoyances. They are no longer able to exert control over your thoughts and feelings. You will feel liberated.

OVERCOME ENVY

I know that I will not take what I cannot give, so I send thoughts of peace, love, and light to ______ and all others. God guides me. I shift my focus away from what ______________ has to what I want, including ______ (describe the things you would like to have for yourself, like health, prestige, income, a spouse, or some other possessions). My blessings can satisfy my needs without seeking those things that others enjoy. According to the law of attraction, everything I want is attracted to me.

Commentary: Never, in any circumstance, should you covet the job of a spouse or someone else's home, job, or anything else. To lust after or envy someone else and their blessings can lead to loss, insecurity, and limitations on yourself. You are reducing yourself in every aspect through such thoughts. You are saying to yourself, "He can have these things, but I cannot." With these words or ideas, you deny the divinity of yourself.

The act of stealing from someone else is stealing from yourself. You could feel the loss in various ways, including negative impacts on your health, popularity, promotions, or love life. You are not interested in being in the same position as your colleague. You may want an identical situation with the same rights such as emoluments, salaries, and other perks. Infinite intelligence could provide a fresh avenue for all of these blessings. If you make a call to it, you will receive an answer.

OVERCOME PROCRASTINATION

The actions I take are a result of thinking. I know what has to be accomplished, and I will achieve it promptly. I am efficient, well-organized, and focused. I prioritize my tasks for the day and execute them in their order of importance or timeliness. I am eager to tackle the most challenging tasks. I possess the skills and abilities needed to finish all of my undertakings and be determined to face any challenge. I am incredibly proud of my achievements and grateful for the abundance of blessings that I receive because of them.

Commentary: Starting a task or project is often the hardest step. Take a few minutes after the conclusion of your day to make your list of things to do for tomorrow. While you drift off to sleep, look towards the day ahead and be grateful for having a plan and goal. Your morning will be filled with an awareness of your focus and direction. Once you have completed each step of your work, check them off your list to celebrate your achievements. Do not leave home without making a plan for the next day.

IMPROVE YOUR ATHLETIC PERFORMANCE

I am relaxed; I am poised; I am serene. The fitness and preparation I have undergone have prepared me for this endeavor. I am at peace before each competition, and the Almighty Force within me will be in charge. I ask this power to be a part of me and move me. I am thankful for the chance to perform and do so with joy. My performance is smooth, flawless, beautiful, and effortless.

Commentary: When gifted athletes achieve a remarkable performance, they typically refer to the experience as being "in the zone." They feel a sense of superhuman power and can perform feats that appear to go above what is humanly possible, doing so seemingly without conscious effort. If you are in the zone, you lose self-confidence. You lose your ego. You are entirely engaged in the action itself and part of the universe. Therefore, your performance will feel effortless, like a more significant force is in charge—and it is. Repeat this affirmation before your athletic events, and you will be able to transfer your performance onto the Almighty power.

SPEAK PUBLICLY WITH CONFIDENCE

I radiate peace, love, and goodwill to all who listen. Love from all over the world surrounds them, wraps them in it, and then envelopes them. I am content to be here and happy to address a subject that I am enthusiastic about. The topic is one in which I am an expert. Infinite intelligence is a force that thinks, talks, and does things through me. My words are capable of healing as well as blessing and inspiration. Peace fills the hearts of all who listen; they are lifted and invigorated with my messages.

Commentary: The fear of speaking in public often prevents people from realizing their maximum potential. To overcome public speaking anxiety and improve confidence, take time to work on your presentation or speech. Repetition of affirmations is not a substitute for planning. Utilize the assertion to relax as you focus on the audience. When you show kindness and affection to the audience before and during your speech or presentation, you will begin to view them as active participants during the event and, therefore, less of a threat.

IMPROVE YOUR PERFORMANCE IN SCHOOL

I have realized I am a treasure trove of memories. My mind effectively stores all the information I have read or learned about from my professors. I have a great memory, and the infinite intelligence within my subconscious mind continually provides me with everything I must know for exams, whether oral or written. I show love and respect to my teachers and classmates.

Commentary: Academic inequities are typically caused by disdain or anger towards colleagues or teachers. Before going to bed and waking up in the morning are the most effective occasions to imbue the unconscious mind with your affirmations. Imagine your parents and teachers praising you for your academic accomplishments. In time, you will see an improvement in your grades and the performance of your class.

IMPROVE YOUR CAREER/BUSINESS SUCCESS

The employees of our company are honest, sincere, loyal, cooperative, and full of kindness to everyone. They are a spiritual and mental connection to its expansion, well-being, and prosperity. I exude peace and love through my words, thoughts, and actions to my coworkers and all employees of the organization. God guides managers and our executives throughout their work. The infinity of my subconscious mind guides all decisions for me. Only right actions are allowed in all of our business dealings and our relationships with one another. I invite the message of love, peace, and goodwill into our offices. Peace and harmony rule the hearts and minds of everyone within the organization, including myself. I can now begin an exciting new day filled with faith, confidence, and focus.

Commentary: Resentment in the workplace can affect your performance and how colleagues and supervisors treat you. The ability to retrain your mind to be optimistic about your contribution to the company and its role in helping to make it successful will result in improved workplace performance and more significant growth for your company as a whole.

IMPROVE RELATIONSHIPS WITH COWORKERS

I do my thinking, speaking, and acting with love, always humbly and calmly. I radiate peace, love, compassion, tolerance, and kindness to those who judge me and make fun of me. I base my thoughts around harmony, peace, and love for all. If I am about to respond negatively, I declare to myself with confidence, "I am going to think, speak, and act in the light of health, harmony, and peace within me. Creative intelligence guides in governing and directs me in all my actions."

Commentary: If you notice that a few employees at your workplace cause you to feel uncomfortable, the noise of annoyance, anger, and agitation could be due to an unconscious pattern or mental projection from you. We all know that dogs can react unusually when encountering someone afraid of or who hates dogs. Animals sense the vibrations of your subconscious and respond to them. People who are not disciplined are just as sensitive to these vibrations as dogs, cats, and other animals. Sometimes, the best method to alter how people behave towards you is to change how you view and treat them.

IMPROVE RELATIONS WITH YOUR SUPERVISOR

I am the sole thinker in my world. I am accountable for what I say about my manager. My boss is not responsible for what I think about her. I am not willing to grant the power to anyone or any place to disturb or annoy me. I wish my boss health, prosperity, peace of mind, and joy. I wish her the best of luck and know that God will guide her throughout her journey, just as He guides me.

Commentary: If there are tensions between you and your superior at work, you likely have feelings of anger and hostility toward this person. Your head is likely full of mental arguments, recriminations, and rebukes of this individual. This means that you are likely to receive back the negativity you have transmitted mentally.

To enhance your relationships with others, say this affirmation loudly, in a calm and slow tone, and with conviction. Believe that your mind is the garden and that what you put on the ground will be the fruits of your thoughts. You can also practice meditation before bed by visualizing your boss congratulating you for your outstanding work enthusiasm and for her having received lovely compliments from customers. Be aware of the reality of this as you feel the handshake of your manager, hear the tone of her voice, and see her smile. Create a mental film by reenacting you to the highest of abilities. Play this film repeatedly in your mind, night after night, and be aware that the subconscious is the receptive plate to your imagination.

SEE PROJECTS THROUGH TO COMPLETION

I have realized that I am part of the incomparable power of my unconscious mind, which does not face any difficulty, obstacle, or slowdown. I am living in the joyful expectation of the most outstanding achievements. My subconscious mind responds to the thoughts I have. I am confident that my infinitely powerful subconscious is unstoppable. Infinite intelligence is always successful, regardless of where it began. My creative wisdom is at work in bringing my ideas and objectives to fulfillment. Whatever I begin, start, I finish, always getting it to a satisfying conclusion. My goal with my job is to offer fantastic service. I hope that my services bless all my contacts. Everything I do comes to its fullest in divine order.

Commentary: If you have difficulty completing projects, closing deals, or delivering on commitments or deadlines, you may be suffering from an internal blockage that stops you from completing tasks until the very end, or you may be functioning amidst the fear that people might withdraw. Persistence is essential to succeed.

EXCEL AS A TEACHER

God has granted me no fear. Instead, he has given me power and love, as well as a clear mind. I have a strong trust that I can count on God as my abundant and ever-present blessing. I am blessed and thriving in all ways. Peace is mine right now. I spread love and positivity to my students, the department head, the school administration, the board, my fellow teachers, and everyone in my life. I wish them all peace and joy from my deepest heart. The wisdom and insight of God inspire and sustain everyone who is in my classes at all times, and I am illuminated and amazed! I immediately consider God's healing love when tempted to form negative thoughts.

Commentary: A teacher once told me she had no success with her class, even though she regularly prayed for success and prosperity. While talking to her, I realized that she was constantly rehearsing her problems in a hostile and accusatory manner, blaming students, parents, and even the school's management and administration. I made it clear to the woman that she was spending the precious resources of her life on negative, destructive thoughts. She changed her outlook and state of mind by repeating the above affirmation regularly with profound awareness. Within a few months, she had established peace in her interactions and earned the promotion.

BUILD AND GROW YOUR BUSINESS

My profession or business is full of correct actions and expressions. The concepts, ideas, knowledge, contacts, and expertise I require are always mine. These things are all magnets for me because of the universal law of attraction. God is the reason for my business. I am guided by God and enthused in every way. Every day, I receive excellent opportunities to expand, grow and advance. I am building trustworthiness. I have accomplished extraordinary achievements because I do business with people the same way I want them to do business with me.

Commentary: A profitable business is just an idea or plan executed well. Many people are scared to begin a business because they fear they are not equipped with the skills required to implement their strategies effectively. This statement can help you draw the ideas, funds, personnel, and contacts you need to start and expand your business. A sincere desire and a firm conviction that your business will succeed when paired with perseverance will result in the success you desire.

PROTECT YOUR HOME, BUSINESS, AND POSSESSIONS

The overshadowing power that guides the planets along their path and makes the sun shine watches over my belongings, including my home, business, and other things that are my own. God is my source of food. My supply is perfect right now. His riches are flowing to me at no cost, in a plethora of ways, and great abundance. I am constantly aware of my worth. I share my talents for free and have been blessedly, divinely paid. Thank you, Father!

Commentary: By constantly reminding yourself of this awe-inspiring truth and observing the rules of love, you will always be directed, monitored, and successful in all ways. You will not suffer loss because you have selected the highest power as your counselor and guide. God's love surrounds and encircles you all the time. You are in the eternal loving arms of God.

OVERCOME IRRATIONAL FEARS

This anxiety has nothing to do with thought and self-deceit. I control my thoughts. I visualize myself as if I am in the presence of the thing or some action. I am at peace.

Commentary: A rational fear is a good thing. You hear the sound of a car speeding across the road, and you take a step back to stay safe. Your actions dispel the fear of being hit. Your parents, relatives, teachers, and everyone who influenced your childhood handed you many irrational fears. These fears are either false or highly exaggerated notions, such as the idea that snakes of all kinds pose a grave danger. The reality is that most snakes are not harmful in any way and will try to avoid you as much—or more—as you do them.

Ralph Waldo Emerson, philosopher, and poet, wrote, "Do the thing you are afraid to do, and the death of fear is certain." Begin by picturing yourself facing the thing you are afraid of repeatedly. For instance, if you fear water, walk down to the pool, gaze at the water and yell out in a loud voice, "I am going to dominate you. I will be able to besiege you." Then, go to the water and take swimming lessons, if needed. Remember that you are the water's master. Do not let the water rule you. If you adopt a new mental attitude, the all-powerful subconscious will respond with strength, confidence, faith, and courage, empowering you to conquer your fears.

OVERCOME TEST ANXIETY

I am aware that my mind's subconscious is a repository of memories. It stores everything I learn from my professors and read about in my books. I have a flawless memory, and the infinite mental capacity of my subconscious continuously reveals everything I must know for any of my exams, whether oral or written. I show love and respect to my teachers and my fellow students.

Commentary: When taking tests or writing academic papers, students are often surprised to discover that their entire knowledge feels as if it is suddenly gone. They cannot think clearly or remember anything about the exam topic. The more they grind their teeth and invoke the strength of their will, the further the answers seem to drift. When they have finally quit the exam, and the pressure on their minds decreases, the solutions they had been searching for immediately surface in their minds. In the end, trying to force themselves to remember was the root of their inability to do just that. This is an example of the universal law, where you receive precisely the things you prayed.

MAINTAIN POISE WHEN THREATENED

I am aware of my surroundings. I am sure that no fear will take root in my head unless I emotionally engage with the idea and accept it as a mental image. I will not entertain any other person's thoughts of fear. So, I am not afraid of harm as I know it will not befall me. I am at work and rest in the calm, deep sea of peace in the center of my being.

Commentary: While doing brand auditing around the globe, I had a 2-hour conversation with a well-known government official. He had a profound feeling of inner peace and calm. He stated that all the criticism he receives from the media and opposition party does not bother his peace. His method is to sit for fifteen minutes each morning and then envision that there is a vast, calm, and peaceful ocean within his being. Meditating gives him tremendous strength to overcome all kinds of challenges and fears.

CALM A TROUBLED MIND

I now declare for ______________ that the wisdom, intelligence, and peace of God is manifested within him and that he is happy, bright, and joyful. He is now covered in the right way. The mind of God is the only genuine and permanent mind. It is the mind of ___________, and he is poised, calm, and at peace. He has faith in God and his life and everything good. I have decided and feel this, and I see him as whole and complete now. Thank you, Father!

Commentary: If you pray for someone who has a mental illness, it is not always possible to get that person's support. The person may have lost the ability to discern and reason. In reality, he is controlled by ghosts from the subconscious, wandering through the dark and gloomy vistas in his brain. If you wish to pray for the person, taking on the entire task yourself is essential. It will help convince you that he is free, in peace, and that you and he are full of harmony and compassion. Repeat this affirmation two or three times per day, with love, affection, and faith in the fact that your beloved one is improving.

In repeating these principles to yourself and realizing that there is only one mind, you will gradually, through the repetition of images within your mind, arrive at a prevailing conviction, and the person you are asking to be healed will, at that moment, be healed.

REMAIN YOUTHFUL

Life is flowing through me like electricity moving through a wire. It is a constant energy source that continually energizes and revitalizes my body and mind. I eagerly anticipate every new day, which offers me the chance to grow and enjoy the world's beauty around me. I am always open to learning more about the wonders of the universe as they unfold to me. My expertise and knowledge enable me to face challenges preventing me from achieving my dreams. I am strong, resilient, vibrant, and unstoppable.

Commentary: The mind of your subconscious never gets old. It is forever, eternal, and never-ending. It is part of the mind of all beings and power that was never born and will not die. Fatigue and old age cannot be attributed to spiritual power or quality. The qualities of patience, kindness, honesty, humility, goodwill, peace, harmony, and brotherly love will never age. If you continue to cultivate these characteristics here on the level of existence and beyond, you will remain youthful in spirit.

COMMIT TO POSITIVE THINKING

From now on, I will open my brain for consumption of only the thoughts and ideas that strengthen, bless, motivate, and build me up.

Commentary: The Bible's ancient wisdom revealed that "As a person imagines and feels, so does she become." This ancient wisdom has been lost in the darkness of time, abandoned in the ages of antiquity. Pyotr Demianovich Ouspensky, a Russian mathematician and esoteric philosopher emphasized the importance of self-talk, or inner speech because inner feelings lead to external behavior. Are you able to speak in a pleasant tone? Your words, silent thought, and feelings align with your goals. Ouspensky's pupil often said, "Watch your inner talking, and let it agree with your aim." The desire and the feeling that are merged through a mental marriage is an answer to prayer.

Write Your Affirmation to Counter a Negative or Destructive Thought

Commentary: Other people might have planted self-defeating and negative thoughts in your mind throughout your life, including: "You will fail," "You have not got a chance," "You are all wrong," "It is no use," "It is not what you know, but whom you know," "The world is going to the dogs," "What is the use? Nobody cares," "It is no use trying so hard," "You are too old now," "Things are getting worse and worse," "Life is an endless grind," "Love is for the birds," "You just cannot win," "Pretty soon you will be bankrupt," "Watch out, you will get the virus," and, "You cannot trust a soul."

Find a destructive or harmful thought that you have implanted in your mind, write your affirmation in response to it, and then utilize your autosuggestion (repeating this affirmation) for replacing the wrong idea with a positive one. Recondition your mind in this manner to restore positive thoughts and behavior.

The Ritual

Power Circle — Imagined

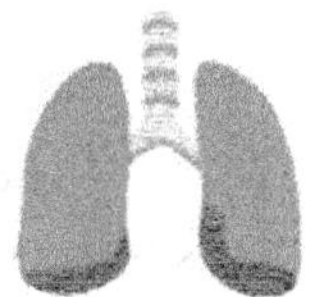

DIVING DEEPER INTO THE SUBCONSCIOUS"

As we wind down, I want to close by sharing several proven methods to help those interested in diving more deeply into the subconscious mind.

To make this as straightforward as possible, I will divide this chapter into two sections:

a) Self-help Methods
b) Therapeutic Methods

SELF HELP METHODS
Let's talk first about self-help methods. These are more in-depth ways to use your relationship with your subconscious mind to improve your life and overall wellbeing. We will take a look at the most popular among them.

Meditation
Most people view meditation as a form of silent sitting, perhaps while listening to a recorded voice or spoken meaningful thoughts against a background of calming music. However, it

is essential to note that this only offers a glimpse into the reality of what meditation is all about. Meditation is truly so much more than this, and the sheer number and effectiveness of its benefits can be mind-boggling.

Meditation is not a single methodology. Instead, there are countless meditations, just as mindsets and psychological needs. It is important to meditate in the way that will best meet your needs and improve your life.

For example, feel free to try a dancing meditation, a flame-starring meditation, a Zen meditation, or the famous gratefulness meditation, to name just a few. Just be sure to select the one—or several—that benefit you the most. Learning what works best for you may take some time, trial, and error.

Meditation is one of my favorite tools to use for centering oneself. Visit a meditation class where they teach different forms to discover the ones which work best for you. Interestingly, some types combine true meditation with self-hypnosis, despite having two other practices. Dr. Joe Dispenza, for example, is famous for his progressive self-hypnosis therapies called "Meditations."

To avoid confusion, we will look at the difference between meditation and hypnosis or self-hypnosis.

On which wave is your brain surfing?
Let's talk about brain frequencies or brain waves. Brain waves are produced when neurons in your brain communicate with each other. They are synchronized electrical pulses of which

different types are created whenever you experience thoughts, emotions, and act out behaviors. Additionally, brain waves differ according to your mood and activity. Slower brain waves make you feel tired and lethargic, whereas higher frequency brain waves make you more alert and active.

Different parts of the brain are stimulated in a particular manner during meditation, causing these extraordinary reactions:

1. The frontal lobe, which plans and reasons, switches off during mediation, helping you detach and relax.

2. The thalamus, which relays motor and sensory signals to the cerebral cortex, slows down its activity, enabling you to keep calm.

3. The parietal lobe, which provides your sense of time, slows down, helping to lower your stress and anxiety levels,

4. The reticular, which keeps your brain alert and helps you respond to situations as they arise, slows down, allowing you to stay calm and be peaceful.

Now that you've seen the power that meditation has over the individual parts of the brain, let's learn about the different types of brain waves:

1. Alpha Waves—Range 9-12 Hz
   Alpha waves are the most common brain waves to occur at the beginning of mediation as you try to move into a deeper

state of mind. They lower the heart rate blood pressure, decrease the production of stress hormones and promote relaxation.

2. Beta Waves—Range 12-30 Hz
   Beta waves become active when your brain is working on goal-oriented tasks. These waves create a more heightened awareness and improve concentration. They increase logical thinking and develop your conversational abilities.

3. Theta Waves - Range 4-8 Hz
   Theta waves are often associated with the concept of "the third eye." Theta waves help us tap into our wisdom, according to spiritual teaching. They become most predominant when we are in the process of completing any task that comes automatically to us, like driving, washing clothes, shampooing hair, folding clothes, and so on. They are also present during the state of daydreaming. Theta waves provide a positive mental state and encourage creativity.

4. Gamma Waves—Range above 30 Hz
   Gamma waves are associated with intense focus. They decrease anxiety and fear while increasing positive emotions. They also reduce depressive feelings and symptoms.

5. Delta Waves—Range of 0-4 Hz
   Delta waves are high amplitude brain waves associated with the deepest stages of sleep. Delta waves increase the production of two anti-aging hormones, DHEA and melatonin. They also help promote deep compassion empathy for others and improve social intelligence.

With so many different brain waves at work during the process of meditation, the benefits of implementing some form of practice into your life are massive and numerous.

1. Increase Gray Matter
   Although there is no conclusive scientific proof of this yet, significant studies have shown that meditation is linked to more substantial amounts of gray matter in the brain's frontal areas. More gray matter can increase focus and emotional stability.

An MRI study conducted at Harvard University showed that meditation leads to thicker gray matter in the parts of the brain that are associated with compassion and self-awareness.

2. Anxiety
   Numerous neural pathways emerge from the medial prefrontal cortex of the brain.

Meditation essentially loosens these tight connections to ensure no strong reactions are triggered in the prefrontal cortex. Meditation reduces pangs of anxiety.

3. Resilience
   Researchers at the University of Wisconsin—Madison took MRI images of the brains of Tibetan monks and discovered that meditation and resilience have a deep-rooted connection.

The study shows that meditation helps the amygdala, or the part of the brain associated with emotion and emotional memories, recover quickly from trauma or stress.

4. Stress

   Reduced stress levels and the release of fewer hormones associated with stress are some of the most significant and most sought-after benefits of deep meditation.

5. Creativity

   At Leiden University, Netherlands, researchers found that people who regularly practice meditation performed better at tasks that demanded divergent thinking.

6. Memory

   The Osher Research Center for Biomedical Imaging determined that people practicing meditation could adjust their brain waves to tune out distraction. This ability is associated with higher productivity and a more straightforward incorporation of new information.

Autosuggestions and Self-hypnosis

We discussed autosuggestions in a previous chapter of this book. Autosuggestions can act as a potent tool when practiced regularly—as long as the autosuggestions are based on your beliefs and are firmly rooted in things that the subconscious will accept. If you copy the suggestions of a mindfulness celebrity word-for-word, but the ideas are not based on you, the process will not work.

The practice of self-hypnosis can be trained and learned by using a hypnosis coach. After trying the methods they teach a few times, you will experience a light trance, Alpha, and you will be able to reload your subconscious.

While there are many techniques for meditation, implementing autosuggestions, and using self-hypnosis on the market now, in a nutshell, it all comes down to acquiring a basic understanding and knowledge of the processes.

These self-help methods are practical and differ mainly only by their technique and marketing.

THERAPEUTIC METHODS

If you look, you will find a massive market full of therapeutic methods, all of which claim to heal your unconscious mind and empower you. However, if you take a deeper look into all of them, you will find that these methods can be reduced to three primary forms.

1. Psychiatric treatment

If you are dealing with serious psychological issues or a psychiatric disorder, please visit a professional. Don't experiment with the methods discussed in this book or any others you may encounter, as it can cause more damage than good. Instead, find a good practitioner through recommendations. Word of mouth often provides the best and most accurate reviews. Find the one that seems right, and give the practitioner a chance to heal your mind.

2. *Brain Spotting* by David Grand

An experienced psychotherapist from New York, David Grand, discovered the power of brain spots while working with a female athlete. What is brain spotting? Well, Grand watched his patient's eye movements and realized a direct and highly intense connection between our eyes and our deep brain.

He realized that the eyes and brain are connected and uncovered a method to dive directly into the brain through eye movement fixation. The look is a direct channel into the deep brain regions. Now his approach has been proven and is utilized by certified practitioners around the globe.

3. Hypnotherapy

As you know, we talked a lot about hypnotherapy and its benefits in this book. In summary, for me, hypnotherapy acts as a shortcut to the subconscious. It has the power to heal and can allow you to grow to your fullest and best potential.

Identity

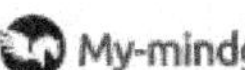

Actual Sorry Identity

Future Positives

My-mindguide.com

Hypnotherapeutic Instruments

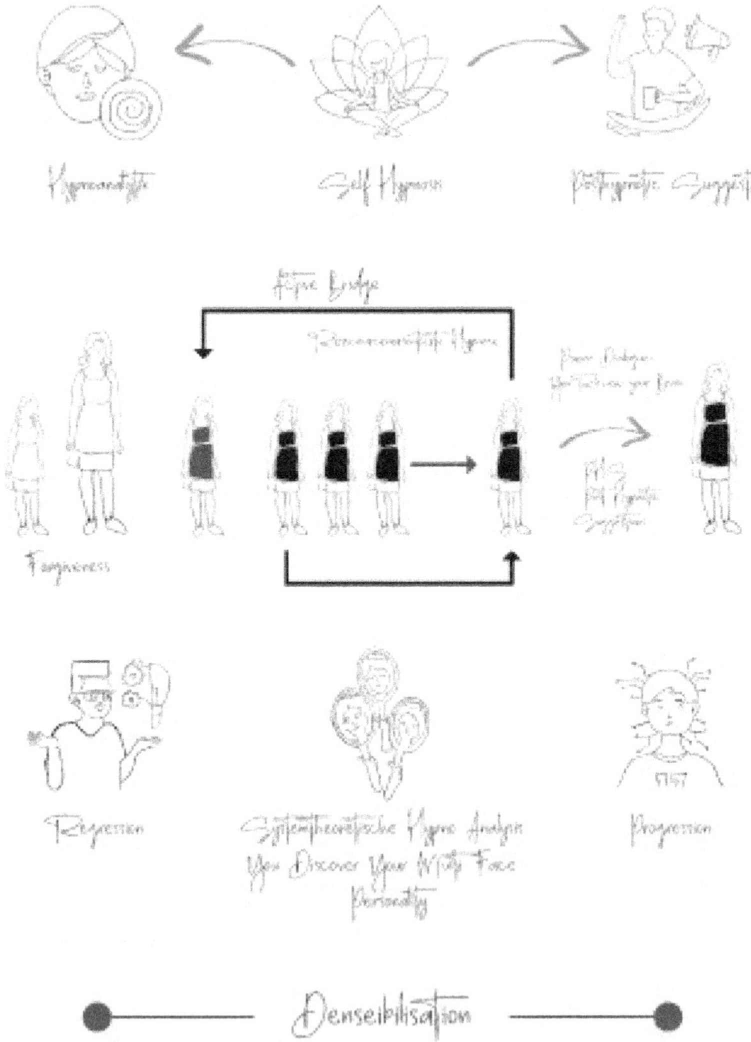

My-mindguide.com

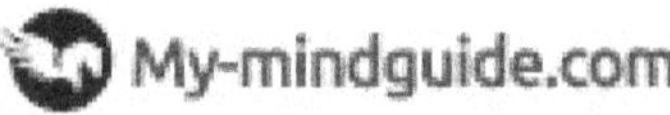

Conclusion:

The word subconscious means below awareness. This mind level is not well defined or understood, but it has tremendous power over human perception and behavior. Almost all brain activity takes place on the subconscious level. Estimates vary, but perhaps only a mere ten percent of information reaches the conscious mind. As Freud put it, "The conscious mind may be compared to a fountain playing in the sun and falling back into the great subterranean pool of subconscious from which it rises."

One of the most challenging parts about assessing the subconscious is that the moment a thought is actively considered, it is no longer subconscious but somewhat conscious. You cannot rely on someone remembering something to understand the subconscious.

Did you know that your **subconscious mind** contains a **limitless supply** of creativity, full stored information, and a vast amount of untapped potential?

Would you like to have **subconscious mind power,** with benefits like:

- The ability to **heal yourself** from the inside out?
- A greater sense of **empathy** & understanding for others?
- Remembering everything in **greater detail?**
- Super-easy access to **life solutions?**
- **Creative abilities** you never dreamed possible?
- Dramatically enhanced **learning abilities?**
- A version of the **root of your fears** & phobias?
- **Clarity of thought** at all times?
- And many more **subconscious mind benefits**...

What's the very best way to reach my subconscious mind so that I can access these benefits? **Merging the state of mind you are currently in, your conscious mind, with the power of your subconscious mind, where these limitless benefits reside, meditation, hypnotherapy, and self-hypnosis are the keys to unlocking the power of your unconscious mind.**

Healing The Past

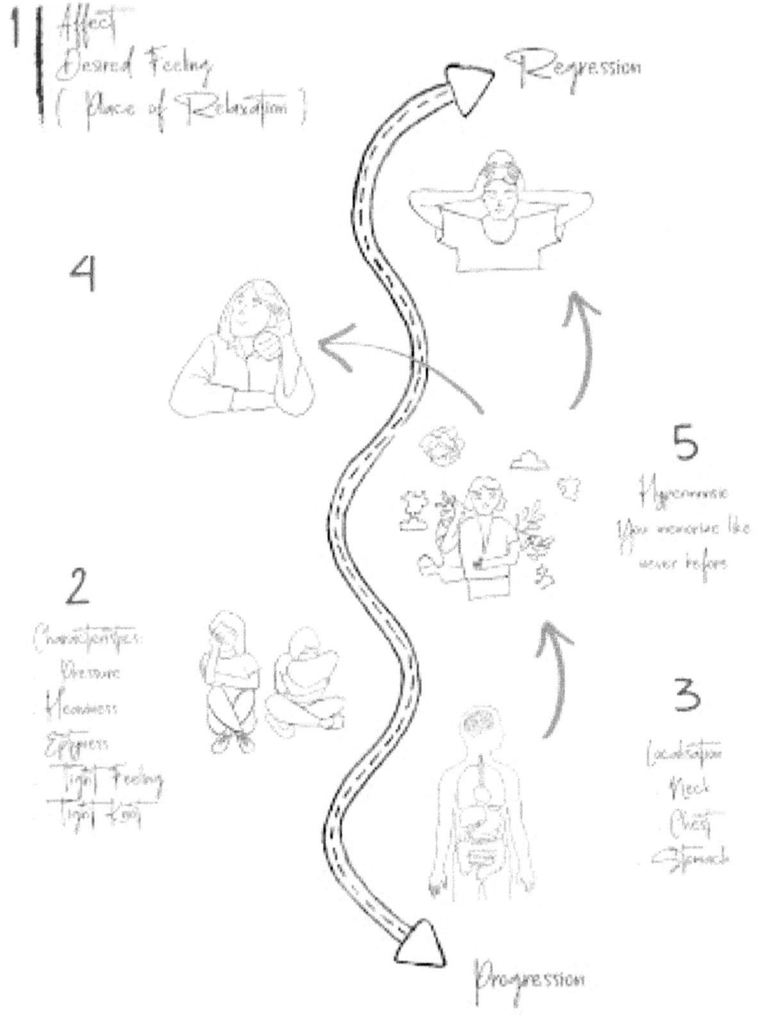

1 | Affect
Desired Feeling
(Place of Relaxation)

Regression

4

2
Characteristics:
Pressure
Heaviness
Emptiness
Tight Feeling
Tight Knot

5
Hypermnesie
Your memories like
never before

3
Localisation
Neck
Chest
Stomach

Progression

FINAL NOTES

If you enjoyed this title and would like to read about other topics that have changed my life, please check out my new books on Amazon or my website: www.my-mindguide.com.

Also, let's stay connected on social media. Please drop a line on Facebook or Instagram, and stay tuned for updates! You're welcome to share your thoughts with me directly as well: gassner@my-mindguide.com. In return, I'll send you a gorgeous infographic that you can cut out and frame.

Also, please leave a review on Amazon, as this will help me reach an even broader audience. Thank you so much for your time, insight, and an undying hunger for knowledge!

I want to thank all of my colleagues, clients, friends, and family members, who have all contributed, in one way or another, to who I am today.

I also want to thank Gabriel Palacios, the king of hypnotherapy and a bestselling Swiss author. They taught this old dog new tricks, letting me deep-dive into the mystery of hypnotherapy.

I learned so much along the journey that I'm now a certified master-hypnosis and conversation coach myself!

Furthermore, I want to thank you to the fantastic teachers of SAMYANA/Bali who trained me to become a certified yoga and meditation instructor.

Last but certainly not least, I give special thanks to my master-teacher Eckhard Wunderle, who is close to a saint to me. He introduced me to the world of meditation and let me discover all the wonders it has to offer. I couldn't be more proud of receiving my meditation teacher certification directly from him at the Institut für Spirituelle Psychologie.

Peace, love, and happiness to all of you—until next time!

Kurt Friedrich Gassner (Signature)

Authors portrait

Kurt Friedrich Gassner has worn many hats throughout his lifetime, including but not limited to serial entrepreneur, Creative Director, Meditation Teacher, Licensed Hypnotherapist, and more recently, self-improvement author. Leveraging his treasure trove of experiences and in-depth knowledge of psychology, he provides his readers with the tools they need to unlock their infinite potential.

As a prolific self-help writer, Kurt has authored the following books: *The Art of Forgiveness, Lie or Die, Soul-Match, Can You Inherit a Poisoned Mind?* and *The Power of Poverty*. He also authored a best-selling children's book in German-speaking countries and has over 20 books underway.

When it comes to enduring success, Kurt understands that financial prosperity isn't the only aspect one should strive for. He may be a self-made millionaire, but what really transformed his life is mastering his unconscious mind. Perseverance, personal power, self-awareness, and learning from past mistakes have all been key ingredients to bringing his dreams to fruition—and he strives to impart that wisdom onto others through his writing.

During his spare time, Kurt Friedrich Gassner is either traveling across the globe, golfing, biking in the Alps, hiking, or spending quality time with his loved ones. For the last 37 years, he has been happily married and he is the father of two successful children. Presently, he resides in both Munich, Germany, and Kirchberg, Austria.

OTHER BOOKS BY THE AUTHOR

My-mindguide.com
Ein praktischer Leitfaden zur
Selbstheilung und zur
Überwindung vergangener
Traumata
Die Kunst Der
VERGEBUNG
KURT GASSNER

My-mindguide.com
SEELEN
VERWANDT
WIE MAN DIE KRAFT DES UNTERBEWUßTSEINS
FÜR SEINE BEZIEHUNGEN NUTZT
KURT GASSNER

My-mindguide.com
Schizophrenes
Leben
Wie man mit einem schizophrenen harmonisch leben kann
KURT GASSNER

My-mindguide.com
Ein inspirierendes Buch zur Überwindung vergangener Traumata
KRAFT DER
VERGEBUNG
SELBSTVERGEBUNG HEILT
KURT GASSNER

My-mindguide.com
Passt
Du zu
Mir?
Wie wir swipen lernen, ohne uns zu verletzen
KURT GASSNER

OTHER BOOKS BY THE AUTHOR

OTHER BOOKS BY THE AUTHOR

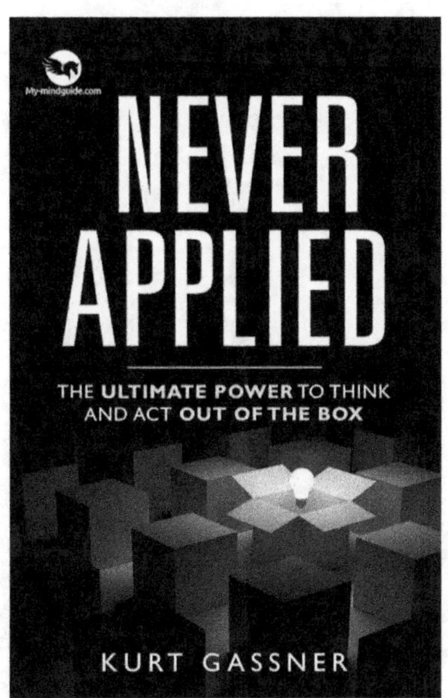

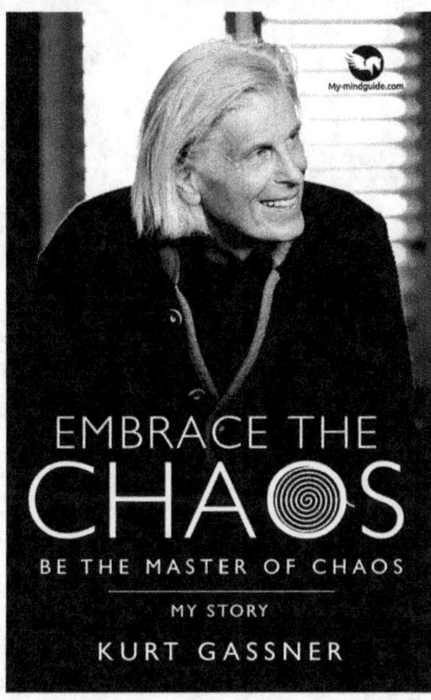

BESTSELLING AUTHOR OF
The Art Of
FORGIVNESS
AMAZON #1 BESTSELLER
My-mindguide.com
A practical guide for self healing and overcome past traumas
The Art Of
FORGIVNESS
KURT GASSNER